Other books in the Jossey-Bass Public Administration Series:

Benchmarking for Best Practices in the Public Sector

Benchmarking for Best Practices in the Public Sector

Achieving Performance Breakthroughs in Federal, State, and Local Agencies

Patricia Keehley
Steven Medlin
Sue MacBride
Laura Longmire

Jossey-Bass Publishers • San Francisco

Substantial discounts on bulk quantities of Jossey-Bass books are available to corporations, professional associations, and other organizations. For details and discount information, contact the special sales department at Jossey-Bass Inc., Publishers (415) 433–1740; Fax (800) 605–2665.

For sales outside the United States, please contact your local Simon & Schuster International Office.

Manufactured in the United States of America on Lyons Falls Pathfinder Tradebook. This paper is acid-free and 100 percent totally chlorine-free.

Credits are on page 252.

Library of Congress Cataloging-in-Publication Data

Keehley, Patricia
    Benchmarking for best practices in the public sector : achieving performance breakthroughs in federal, state, and local agencies / Patricia Keehley . . . [et al.]. — 1st ed.
       p.   cm. — (The Jossey-Bass public administration series)
    Includes bibliographical references and index.
    ISBN 0-7879-0299-3
    1. Total quality management in government—United States.
    2. Benchmarking (Management)—United States. I. Title.
    II. Series.
JK468.T67K44   1996
350′.00068′4—dc20

                                           96-10092
                                            CIP

HB Printing 10 9 8 7 6 5 4 3 2 1   FIRST EDITION

The Jossey-Bass
Public Administration Series

Contents

Foreword

Governments are going through a major transformation as the nation moves from an industrial society to an information society. You can see the signs in everyday events: you use an ATM card to get cash . . . the cashier scans your purchases at the grocery store . . . you make an electronic payment on a toll road . . . your child does her homework over the Internet.

As people become more accustomed to this kind of instantaneous, high-quality response, they are less likely to accept the long delays and red tape that have often characterized government services. In fact, they are already demanding that government act more like a business.

To succeed in this environment, government must act differently—very differently—from the way it has acted in the past. The most farsighted governments understand this pressure and are trying to retool themselves to adapt. But for all the talk of reinventing and reengineering, privatizing and outsourcing, downsizing and rightsizing, quality management and continuous improvement, it is difficult for most governments to get the answers they need to make it happen.

As KPMG has helped states, cities, federal agencies, colleges, universities, and nonprofit organizations through this process, we have found that there are plenty of books on the theory and philosophy of such change but few, if any, guides to practical tools and techniques.

That is what this book is all about. It is a workbook full of proven methods, designed to be used rather than to sit on a shelf in your office. It should be considered successful if it is dog-eared from being passed around among those doing the hard work that real transformation requires.

Fortunately, the public sector does not have to set out blindly on this journey. It can follow the lead of America's leading businesses, which began to make the transition in the 1980s. The course they have charted can help the public sector to successfully navigate the turbulence of change in its own environment. That will mean adapting the private sector model to the complex world of public management—which presents unique pressures and circumstances—rather than adopting it as a whole.

One of the critical tools government can take advantage of is benchmarking, a methodology that shows how to improve performance dramatically by comparing the performance of one's own organization with the best practices of others. Essentially, it provides a map showing where an organization needs to go in order to improve.

By comparing your organization to public or private sector leaders that provide similar services, you can achieve leapfrogging improvements in the way you work. We are not talking about gradual, incremental change but about radical change that produces significant gains in performance.

We have seen how benchmarking can inspire public and private sector organizations, including our own firm, to change. For example, KPMG used benchmarking to help a large pharmaceutical company improve its proposal preparation process. A comparison of our client with other marketing-intensive, regulated industries showed that whereas the client's process took an average of ninety days, their benchmarking partners took one hour! To help the company reach its initial goal of cutting the process to thirty days, we instigated a new process allowing personnel to propose contracts at the customer's site.

Similarly, we have helped government clients ranging from the U.S. Department of Defense to the state of North Carolina and the city of Indianapolis to apply best practices to improve their operations. Through these efforts, our clients are improving basic business processes—such as purchasing, payroll administration, data processing, and running a help desk—and providing useful information to decision makers.

The bottom line is that benchmarking works. This book shows you how to make it work for *you*, in clear, simple terms, backed up by examples drawn from other government organizations. The book is written for all public sector executives, managers, and employees who want to meet—or exceed—their customers' expectations. We hope that elected and appointed officials will also read it, since real change starts from the top. In addition, community leaders and interested citizens can use the information here to encourage public service providers to find and implement best practices.

What is offered in the following pages is a step-by-step methodology for benchmarking. The procedures described can be used to prepare for and conduct a benchmarking project, then to implement the identified best practices and sustain the improved results. Throughout, the political realities of undertaking such an effort in the public eye are addressed.

Overview of the Contents

The book is structured to guide you through the process. Part One discusses issues that must be addressed before beginning a benchmarking project. Chapter One offers criteria for defining a best practice and describes how the criteria apply to various examples from public and private organizations. In Chapter Two, we describe what benchmarking is and—just as important—what it is not. Our experience is that much of what is currently being reported as benchmarking is in fact merely "industrial tourism"— that is, a glimpse of what others are doing. True benchmarking requires a methodology, applied with rigor and discipline. This chapter explores the reasons for benchmarking and outlines what you might expect from your organization as benchmark data begin to be reported.

Chapter Three emphasizes the need for a receptive environment and political climate. A list of criteria are offered to help you conduct an organizational readiness check before moving ahead. Chapter Four helps you target the best candidates for benchmarking. Because no organization can be world class in every process—nor afford to seek out best practices for every function— your organization must decide which processes it wants to improve.

Part Two outlines a detailed methodology of benchmarking and how it can be applied to seek out best practices. Chapter Five explains how you can use this approach to define your process,

find other organizations with best practices in your area of interest, and import the best practice for your organization. Chapter
Six suggests ways to involve stakeholders from the start to generate
ideas and support for your project.

Chapter Seven emphasizes the importance of looking at many
aspects of potential benchmarking partners. It presents selection
criteria, as well as considerations for applying the criteria and
selecting a partner. Chapter Eight includes tips and tools for ensuring a successful partnership, including advice on conducting site
visits, data collection, and other procedures.

Chapter Nine addresses the art of judging when and where to
import practices. In our experience, it is rare that a practice will
be adopted without some adaptation by the importing organization. Using the *gap analysis* method, a case study is presented to
illustrate where best practices would be helpful.

The final two chapters of the book deal with the real challenge:
how to keep the momentum going not only for the new best practice but for the entire benchmarking process. Chapter Ten stresses
the need to carefully plan a strategy for using the project's findings. Chapter Eleven outlines the monitoring process, particularly
the need for ongoing information review, to keep your organization on track.

Ultimately, the power of benchmarking is expressed in the
"Aha!" experience that team members get when they witness a best
practice or innovation. The response is always the same: "We never
thought about doing it that way. Why couldn't we do it?" These
innovations usually lead to even higher levels of improvement,
because they spark new ideas.

As your team implements the best practices in your field, you
will improve on the design or implementation of what went before.
Now *you* are the benchmark. And that's the whole point.

August 1996   LARRY HERMAN
                                 Principal, KPMG Peat Marwick LLP
                                 JACK MILLER
                                 Partner, KPMG Peat Marwick LLP

The Authors

PATRICIA KEEHLEY has over twenty years of public and private sector management experience that includes work on numerous benchmarking projects. She received her B.S. degree in psychology (1977) from the University of South Florida, her Master of Public Administration degree (1983) from the University of South Florida and her Doctor of Public Administration degree (1990) from the University of Georgia.

She began her public sector career in 1983 with the U.S. General Accounting Office, where she spent one year detailed to the U.S. House of Representatives Appropriations Committee staff. From 1989 to 1992 she was a visiting faculty member at the University of Utah, serving as director for public administration education. As a consultant with Coopers & Lybrand she worked with many public sector organizations to implement quality management and performance measurement systems.

In 1994 she founded the iKon Group, inc., a firm that specializes in providing performance improvement services to the public and nonprofit sectors. Her clients include numerous cities, counties, states, and federal agencies. She has delivered numerous training sessions and speeches about public sector organizational performance and has published several articles about quality management and benchmarking.

STEVEN MEDLIN is chief operating officer for iKon Group, inc. He has over seventeen years of experience in the federal sector, where he worked with the Army Research Institute for the Behavioral and Social Sciences, the General Accounting Office, and the Internal Revenue Service (IRS). He received his B.S. degree in mathematics (1972) from Stetson University, and his M.A. (1974) and Ph.D.

(1976) degrees, both in quantitative psychology, from the University of North Carolina.

From 1989 to 1992, he served as the assistant director at the IRS Ogden Service, where he chaired the organization's Quality Council, which won the President's Award for Quality in 1992. As director of systems development at the IRS, his information systems development projects won many national awards for excellence and quality. Medlin has written numerous articles and given many speeches on quality management implementation and organizational performance improvement in the public sector. He is a well-known international writer, trainer, and presenter.

SUE MACBRIDE has over five of years of experience working with government contractors and nonprofit interest groups. She has worked in conjunction with the Massachusetts Women's Caucus, the Boston Water and Sewer Commission, the Department of Housing and Urban Development, and the Department of Veterans Affairs. She received her B.A. degree in political science (1991) from Wellesley College and her Master of Public Administration degree (1996) from the George Washington University, with a concentration in management of state and local governments. MacBride joined the iKon Group in May 1995 as a research associate.

LAURA LONGMIRE currently serves as director of benchmarking for KPMG Peat Marwick LLP. She coordinates, facilitates, and trains for internal business process studies and does benchmarking consulting for KPMG clients.

Longmire received her B.S. degree in biology (1974) from Missouri Southern State College and her M.B.A. degree in contract acquisition and management (1991) from the University of Dallas. She serves as a member of the steering committee for the International Benchmarking Clearinghouse in Houston. She currently teaches benchmarking courses for the Federal Quality Institute, the National Performance Review, and the executive development program of Kellogg Graduate School of Management at Northwestern University. In addition, she serves on the training board and the board for benchmarking competency of the American Society for Quality Control.

Prior to joining KPMG, Longmire was the benchmarking champion of the worldwide operations of Texas Instruments. Within the quality information systems of Texas Instruments, she developed an internal benchmarking library and electronic benchmarking database. She was responsible for deploying benchmarking within Texas Instruments from 1989 to 1994. She has facilitated studies in the areas of product development, manufacturing operations, order entry, diversity management, team recognition and reward, logistics and distribution, cost proposals, and performance reviews. Prior to benchmarking, she was a manufacturing operations manager.

In June 1995, Longmire was selected to testify before the U.S. House of Representatives Committee on Government Reform and Oversight. Her testimony was used to familiarize the committee with performance improvement, benchmarking, and reengineering. She was awarded the 1996 TWIN award for women in industry.

Acknowledgments

As with any other major endeavor, this book is the product of numerous team members who made significant contributions to the end result. We would like to share the success with the team, while remaining solely responsible for the contents, opinions, and any errors that may be found in the book.

The case studies could not have been completed without the energy and enthusiasm of the Reno, Salt Lake City, and West Virginia team members. Thanks to Brenda Hancock, Brad Baxter, Anna Wilson, Pam Witt, Mike Freeland, and Gary Griffiths for all their help. Misty Histeman and Kerri Nakamura provided important support while representing the Salt Lake City Council. The leadership of Bill Thomas, Carol Peterson, and Randy Baxley on behalf of Reno was a model for everyone involved in a benchmarking initiative. Many thanks to Roger Black and Mayor DeeDee Corradini (Salt Lake City) and city manager Clay Holstine (Reno) for recognizing the benefits of looking outside the city for ways to improve. We thank Governor Gaston Caperton of West Virginia for generously sharing information from his benchmarking teams, including the work completed by Carla Dunn, Andrew Brown, and Gary Lanham.

Dottie Disher, in Charlotte, North Carolina, exceeded our highest expectations for a benchmarking host and partner. A bundle of energy and information, she overwhelmed the site visit teams with hospitality, great ideas, and words of encouragement. Terry Wittman in Seattle ensured that our benchmarking visit met and surpassed the needs of all our partners. We thank Terry for responding to our request to meet numerous people within the city.

Many thanks to Tanya Barvenik and Gene Davis of Arlington County, Virginia, who were instrumental in advising us on budding benchmarking projects in their local government. Ron Carlee, director of human services, was always available to answer random questions. Susan Ingraham, zoning administrator, willingly shared her experiences with performance measures. Fire chief Edward P. Plaugher encouraged us with his benchmarking project. Our appreciation also goes to John Scully of the Public Innovator Learning Network at the National Academy of Public Administration and Stewart Umpleby of George Washington University for allowing us to join his benchmarking videoconference.

Grammarians, Inc., and Mellen Candage provided a significant amount of editorial support and personal encouragement that we greatly appreciated. Lyndi Schrecengost demonstrated an exceptional talent for tackling the less focused aspects of the book and providing a meaningful structure for them. Judy Cusick's interest in details was vital to our success and continues to be a skill that amazes us.

As our key client while writing the book, Linda Maldonado with the Federal Deposit Insurance Corporation must be thanked for her patience with us throughout the writing process. Finally, we greatly appreciated the daily support, assistance, and interest from our friends and colleagues: Melissa Johnston, Jon Wijnand, Dianne DiDio, Carolyn Brock, Toni Yowell, and especially James Mintzer.

Arlington, Virginia
August 1996

Patricia Keehley
Steven Medlin
Sue MacBride

How Best Practices Strengthen Public Organizations

Why do government agencies need to use best practices? Thousands of miles of poor and mediocre roads and highways, obsolete bridges, impoverished and overloaded mass transit systems and airports, inferior water supply systems, insufficient sewage treatment facilities, and outdated overreliance on landfills for solid waste are just a sampling of answers to this question. With scarce budget resources, a rapidly deteriorating infrastructure, a growing population, an endangered environment, and a stressed educational system, taxpayers increasingly are demanding greater results for their tax dollars. The search for better ways of producing results has never before been more critical.

Reasons for Benchmarking

As public sector entities begin importing best practices from high-performing organizations, they will be more likely to share strategies on a regular basis with one another, igniting a chain reaction among organizations striving to do better, like synapses firing consecutively in the brain. We want to spread the fire of best practices. To this end, we present seven practical reasons for public administrators to undertake a search for best practices.

1. It Works

The improvements in quality and efficiency that private industry has obtained through best practices and benchmarking have been

1

so profound and widespread that states, counties, cities, nonprofit organizations, and federal agencies—organizations known for their slow pace in planning and implementing change—are waking up to the benefits of this powerful analytical tool (Bruder and Gray, 1994, p. S9). To the surprise of many organizations, benchmarking usually reveals sizable performance gaps. When the Lynchburg, Virginia, fire and emergency medical services did a benchmarking study, the city was found to have a fire death rate 150 percent above the mean. Such findings are to be expected when an agency benchmarks itself against organizational best practices (Gay, 1992, p. 18). (Results from the Lynchburg project are not available. We can only assume that after importing best practices, the fire death rate was brought down closer to the benchmark mean.)

Under the command of General John Michael Loh, the Air Combat Command (ACC) measures its performance against similar units in the U.S. Army, Navy, and Marine Corps, units in other nations' air forces, and even the private sector. Before benchmarking began, the average F-16 refueling took forty-five minutes. Afterward teams were able to decrease the time to thirty-six minutes and then to twenty-eight (National Performance Review, 1993). In the area of performance, General Loh believes that anything that is not measured can never be improved.

Among the well-known private sector efforts, General Motors benchmarked AC Delco Systems's 1996 fuel pump and found three breakthrough improvements: (1) the efficiency of the previous year's model was doubled; (2) the vibration magnitude was reduced by a factor of five; and (3) durability was increased from 4,200 to 10,000 hours (International Institute for Learning, 1995a, p. 13). In another successful benchmarking experience, Cleveland Memorial Hospital reduced unexpected patient arrivals by 9 percent in three months, increased accuracy of patient information by 5 percent, and reduced annual overtime by two hundred hours (International Institute for Learning, 1995a, p. 28).

International benchmarking can also have major benefits. The *koban* is a Japanese police substation, part of the nation's law enforcement policy of stationing officers in the neighborhoods they protect. Under the auspices of the Milton S. Eisenhower Foundation, police chiefs from several U.S. cities visited Japan in 1988 to see how *kobans* work. The first two U.S. cities to institute *kobans* as part of their community policing efforts were Philadelphia and San Juan, Puerto Rico. The results were impressive: a 35 percent decrease in the crime rate between 1989 and 1993 in the San Juan neighborhood where a *koban* was used, and a 24 percent drop in crime between 1991 and 1993 in a retail section of Philadelphia using *kobans*. Several years later, in May 1995, Baltimore officials opened a *koban* in a busy commercial district. The air-conditioned, bulletproof unit in which two officers operate cost only $150,000 to construct. Officers on duty in the *koban* say that crimes common to the area—purse snatching, shoplifting, assaults, and robberies— have declined sharply. Overall, observes Alfred Dean, executive director of the Police Foundation, police departments are finally accepting the fact that at a time when citizens are demanding more from the police despite fewer resources, the old methods are just not working (Janofsky, 1995, p. A8). New and better practices such as the use of *kobans* have made a timely arrival.

2. Recognition Is Likely to Follow

In addition to the internal benefits gained from importing best practices, significant opportunities exist for external, tangible benefits, in the form of remuneration and publicity. Many national and international performance awards exist, with winners determined by their use of best practices. For example, benchmarking to find best practices is required for the Malcolm Baldrige National Quality Award, which will be opened to the public sector sometime after 1997. Currently the Baldrige award application addresses external drivers of organizational improvement by asking for data and information related to competitive position and best practices. Applicants are required to describe how they chose competitive comparisons and benchmarking data and used them to improve process performance and set hard targets for the future (National Institute of Standards and Technology, 1995, p. 7).

Under another Baldrige award requirement, each applicant must submit a description of the procedures it uses to evaluate and improve its process for selecting benchmark data (National Institute of Standards and Technology, 1995, p. 7). In other words, Baldrige award judges want to know what an organization is comparing its performance to and why, what the rationale behind the chosen benchmarks is, and whether the organization is keeping a close eye on the latest developments elsewhere and adapting benchmarks accordingly—or if it is simply reusing the same data year after year. The premises of these criteria are that companies must determine where they stand in relation to their competitors and to the best practices for similar processes and that benchmarking, by alerting companies to new practices, makes breakthrough improvement possible (National Institute of Standards and Technology, 1995, p. 7). When the Baldrige award opens up to public sector organizations, government entities that compete for it will have to practice benchmarking and track practices to determine the best ones, whether they be for issuing licenses or running a health care program.

Best practices are also a requirement for other competitions. Since 1988 the Carl Bertelsmann Prize has been awarded to municipalities that implement innovative, excellent ideas that further the development of democratic societies. In 1994 Phoenix, Arizona, and Christchurch, New Zealand, shared $180,000 as co-recipients of the prize. Along with the money, this special recognition brought streams of visitors, advice seekers, interviewers, and government administrators from around the globe to both cities, all seeking to learn the secret of their success. As competition for this award increases, applicants will no doubt exhibit great skill in finding and importing best practices to maintain innovation and excellence in their cities. Everyone wants to be the best.

3. Other Organizations Have Already Started

Making government more effective and efficient is the national issue of the hour, but getting it to work better for less will not be possible unless governments find ways to work smarter. Unfortunately, unlike the private sector, governments have not kept up with evolving management practices. Falling behind has led to wasted resources, a frustrated citizenry unable to get high-quality service, and agencies unprepared to measure and manage their affairs in a businesslike manner. In response to current and future demand, the best practices approach is already being investigated by several public sector entities, including Salt Lake City, Utah; Reno, Nevada; the West Virginia state government; the U.S. Postal

Service; and the New Jersey court system. Some of these cases will be examined in later chapters.

Agencies that want to identify the best performance in their field must first thoroughly understand their own internal practices. The search for best practices forces organizational introspection, bringing to light the hidden demons, problems, and bugs of the organization. Such self-assessment, like an extended session with a psychotherapist, may be painful, but it is ultimately beneficial.

Once a public agency understands why a performance gap exists between it and the best in class, it can use this knowledge to improve its own program performance ("Innovation Group's Standard Reporting of Performance Measures," n.d., p. 4). For example, when the National Performance Review (NPR) outlined ways—in *From Red Tape to Results: Creating a Government That Works Better and Costs Less* (1993), the "Gore Report"—to improve the use of computers and communications in the federal government, the effort would have failed, according to team member Laraine Rodgers of Phoenix, had it not been for the best practices approach, which "provided some quick points of focus as well as some means for benchmarking the workability of ideas" (Anthes, 1993, p. 4). NPR identified several practices, including the Iowa Communications Network, thousands of miles of fiber-optic cable transmitting data and video to state agencies, schools, and libraries. (Attempts at importing these practices have not yet been reported.)

Even Oregon, recognized to be in the vanguard of the benchmarking movement, has been advised that its approach is not reaching its full potential because the state is looking only internally, not externally, for performance improvement opportunities. This does not mean that progress is not being made. The Alliance for Redesigning Government, a program run by the National Academy of Public Administration (NAPA), has reported that Oregon has achieved important results with its health care strategy, including the immunization of seven thousand children in one day (D. Osborne, in a letter to the authors, 1995). Also, under its emergency preparedness benchmarks, Oregon reduced structural fire damage from $79.2 million in 1989 to $57.2 million in 1993 (Oregon Progress Board, 1994).

In his 1994 assessment of the Oregon benchmarks, John Kirlin of the University of Southern California proposed a new benchmarking strategy for the state. Kirlin recommended that Oregon compare its past and current performance with other states and nations, not just with itself. By adding comparison data to its tables in the categories of national average, best state in America, best nation, and second-best nation, Oregon officials could see more clearly where the state stood in relation to others, which services needed the most improvement, and how Oregon should prioritize its efforts. Oregon Shines (Oregon Economic Development Department, 1989), the state's twenty-year plan, may produce a better place to live, but only in relation to Oregon's historical self, not in relation to other states or nations. If the state continues to limit itself to internal benchmarks while other states adopt best practices, it could find itself slipping in rankings a decade from now. Kirlin's most important piece of advice for Oregon was to "examine the best practices from other states, and especially, from around the world. Look widely for innovative new ways to achieve benchmarks. Don't presume that a goal can only be achieved by spending more money on current programs" (Hatry and Kirlin, 1994, p. 8).

Oregon's goals, which were established through quality management approaches, actually encourage a search for best practices. According to criteria for the Baldrige award, "Strong emphasis on cycle time reduction in all operations encourages agencies to analyze work paths, work organizations, and the value-added contributions of all process steps. This fosters change, innovation, and creative thinking in how work is organized and conducted" (National Institute of Standards and Technology, 1995, p. 17). The search for best practices forces an agency to undertake this type of analytical thinking and thoroughly dissect its own processes. Work needs to be broken down into its most basic elements, in the same manner, say, as the elements making up water—hydrogen and oxygen—can be broken down into protons, neutrons, and electrons. The organizational process is then rebuilt in accordance with the imported practice.

At the federal level, such changes are already being made. The Chief Financial Officers Act, the Government Performance and Results Act, the NPR, and the Paperwork Reduction Act promote financial accountability, implement results-oriented management, modernize operations, and improve information management (General Accounting Office, 1994). The belief in the necessity of best practices has reached all the way to the White House. In 1993

President Clinton signed Executive Order 12862, which instructs government agencies to survey their customers, find out what they want, set service standards accordingly, and measure their services against the "best in the business" (National Performance Review, 1995, p. 1). The idea underlying all of these official acts is that citizens deserve to receive the highest-quality services for their tax dollars. The postal service, for instance, in response to an enduring reputation for inefficiency, has established the following delivery benchmarks: 95 percent of all first-class items sent within 500 miles will arrive in one business day; between 501 and 2,500 miles, they will arrive in two days; and over longer distances, in three days. Postal service officials developed these standards after surveys revealed what customers defined as good service; the standards apply uniformly to offices across the country (Fischer, 1994, p. S3).

As the federal government improves customer service and quality, citizens will no longer put up with state and local jurisdictions that operate in the same old way. Pressure from both the top and the grassroots will catch state or local governments off guard unless they act now.

4. Building on the Work of Others Makes Sense

Invention is not the only way to express ingenuity. Building on or improving on the invention of another is also ingenious, as well as time-saving and cost-effective. When an organization learns from the experiences of others, it greatly reduces both the time required to move up the learning curve and the cost of improvement. For example, in the 1960s Tandy improved on the postwar Electronic Numerical Integrator and Calculator (ENIAC), the first modern, general-purpose electronic computer, weighing thirty tons and measuring eighteen by eighty feet. A decade later Apple improved on the Tandy model. Now several computer manufacturers are vying for the top spot in the business by improving (almost monthly, it seems) on what their competitors are offering. Simply put, superior performance is based on an organization's ability to adopt the industry's best product or service features and to deliver defect-free products and services. Not only do organizations have to do the right thing, but they have to do it right the first time. It is this combination of skill and timing, which sounds so logical and easy but is really difficult and therefore not common, that leads to superior performance (Public Management Group, *Benchmarking Law Enforcement Services,* p. 14). According to Coopers & Lybrand, "Tomorrow's leading organizations are today's innovators" (Coopers & Lybrand, n.d., p. 4).

In the public sector there was little incentive to improve because many government entities had a monopoly on their mousetraps. The dominant perception is that most governments have been plodding along, making incremental steps in improvement throughout their history. Now, shrinking or stable budgets and soaring demands from citizens call for dramatic change. With best practices, public organizations can operate on a higher plane, in a mode more akin to leapfrogging the competition, where the pace of change is faster and the amount of change is greater.

5. You Cannot Afford Not To

Citizens want to receive high-quality service as a return on their tax dollars, just as they do on their purchasing dollars. Increased private sector focus on quality and value has raised citizens' expectations of the public sector (Gay, 1992) and intensified their dissatisfaction. The NPR recognizes that taxpayers are appalled at having to foot the bill for what they perceive as poor service from government agencies (National Performance Review, 1995, p. 1). For instance, anyone can get eyeglasses in about an hour from a retail outfit, but according to the General Accounting Office (GAO) (1994, p. 7), veterans have to wait six weeks to receive them from the Department of Veterans Affairs (VA). If the VA were to benchmark top-performing retail distributors and then import the practices used in these establishments, the result would be a significant reduction in the VA's lag time.

Most public administrators do not want to hear Senator John Glenn (D–Ohio) tell them that there is a "profound feeling across the country that government has not been doing its job" (Fischer, 1994, p. S2). Public administrators are quite aware that frustrated citizens are becoming more vocal about wanting effective and responsive government. Voters object to wasted tax dollars, the government's failure to plan for the nation's future, and the lack of real accountability; they accuse the government of being unresponsive, gridlocked, and too bureaucratic. The current attitude of "Shape up or ship out" was reflected in the November 1994 elections when, out of anger or frustration, voters swept several incumbents out of office. Bertelsmann Foundation chairman Robert Mohn has said, "The need to modernize our public administrations is greater today than ever before, given the squeeze on public spending and the growing dissatisfaction of citizens with inefficient bureaucracy" ("This Year's Carl Bertelsmann Prize," 1993, p. 1). Without immediate action, the gap between public expectations and agency performance will continue to grow, and the pressure of citizen dissatisfaction with it.

Local jurisdictions are also facing unprecedented budgetary pressures as a result of cutbacks at the federal, state, and local levels and efforts in Congress to eliminate or devolve many federally funded programs (Bruder and Gray, 1994, p. S9). Local jurisdictions can expect to be asked to do more with less. Productivity and quality improvement are no longer matters of choice for local administrators. Starting now, organizational success, competitiveness, and stability will be determined by how well and how fast public agencies improve their business processes. Best practices, benchmarking, business process reengineering, and having a customer focus are not just desirable; they are necessities in today's environment (American Productivity and Quality Center, n.d., p. 1).

For several years now, private sector organizations have been looking outside themselves for improvement ideas. Today's successful companies are regarded as such because they have taken an approach that values the successes of others. Motorola's importing of methods from Domino's Pizza and Xerox's study of L. L. Bean's approach to warehouse productivity are among the most often cited examples (Doades, 1992, p. 15). Although public agencies have been collecting program data for years, a comparative performance analysis has never been conducted by government programs on a sustained, large-scale basis, perhaps because the task would not be easy. Unlike private sector organizations, public agency partnerships would have a much harder time reaching consensus on what types of measures to use and on the definition of certain terms, among other hurdles ("Innovation Group's Standard Reporting of Performance Measures," n.d., p. 3). The first of the public sector best practice–benchmarking projects will be especially demanding; agencies or departments first off the starting block will have to break new ground and pave the way for those that follow.

6. It Leads to Cooperation

Other benefits of finding best practices are not as obvious as quality or performance improvement, but they are just as important. For example, NPR found that several federal employees have come together informally and formed BenchNet, a network designed to promote benchmarking within their various agencies. BenchNet, which is developing a database of practices that have promise for the federal government, can be accessed through the FedWorld electronic bulletin board (National Performance Review, 1995, p. 4). The American Society for Quality Control (ASQC) has also established a nationwide network. Its Benchmarking Competency Center has created a dial-up bulletin board, The Benchmarking Exchange (TBE), which allows ASQC members to scan a database on best practices made up of journal citations ("Benchmarking Code of Conduct," 1994, p. 15). A focus on best practices encourages agencies to look outside themselves and can help to form bonds between government and business where before there were none.

Best practices and benchmarking bring together for the first time diverse public functions—human services, criminal justice, and others—to improve the community (Scully, 1995). Agencies, municipalities, and states participating in benchmarking searches for best practices benefit from the communication between one another on important topics of the day, such as crime, homelessness, and downtown revitalization. Katherine Barrett and Richard Greene (1993) discovered the importance of these linkages in their search for America's best-run city programs, detailed in their series of articles, "Focus on the Best," for *Financial World* magazine. The Public Sector Network, a technical committee established by ASQC, fosters collaboration among government entities and also helps government agencies to increase their capacity to deliver services that meet, and even surpass, public expectations (Public Sector Network News, 1994, p. 1). Best practices is proving to be one of the best means for instilling lasting collaboration.

7. Taxpayers Are Viewed as Customers

In the introduction to their articles on best-run cities, Barrett and Greene (1993) cite three great urban myths that have attached themselves to all U.S. cities: "nothing ever gets better," "the only way to make things better is to spend more," and "when you do spend more, things only get worse" (p. 37). The mass adoption of best practices by public sector agencies may eliminate these myths from the media coverage and from the American psyche for good because best practices encourage fresh thinking and expand possibilities.

Behind the search for best practices lies a new way of thinking about the role of government in our society. In the light of increasing citizen distrust and the accompanying movement to restrict government revenues, "astute government officials are beginning to view their constituents as paying customers entitled to responsive service, efficient performance, and a feeling of customer satisfaction for their tax investment" ("Governing for Results," 1994, p. 3). How many people would privately invest such a high percentage of their income in something they did not trust to give them an adequate return? West Virginia's governor, Gaston Caperton, who came to his office from the private sector, observed early in his term that the state government was inefficient in its delivery of services. Realizing that taxpayers were increasingly demanding more "bang for the buck" and that budgets would only keep shrinking, Caperton began to look around for ways of improving government efficiency at no extra cost. Using General Electric as his model, he instituted benchmarking as the second phase of what was to be West Virginia's Inspire Initiative, based on a quality management philosophy. Other government leaders must begin to treat tax dollars as the investment of citizens in the community, not as an endless resource to which the government has a right.

Public leaders who choose to adopt best practices for one or more of the seven reasons understand that government has a critical role to play as a leader and catalyst in helping communities compete in a changing world economy; they also recognize the limits of government as provider. These leaders deal with the reality that governments must become better managers of limited fiscal resources by reallocating funds to higher priorities, curbing problems early on, and providing taxpayers with a more thorough accounting of return on expenditures ("Governing for Results," 1994, p. 4). Successful leaders receive the greatest return on their investment by capitalizing on available tools and methods such as best practices and benchmarking. That is the secret to maintaining leadership and performance in the face of constant change.

Benchmarking and the Public Sector

This is a process book. Our purpose is to describe benchmarking as it applies to the public sector and to promote its use. The concentration on process is what distinguishes our treatment from other, similar books. We have avoided a statistical textbook format and a discussion filled with technical jargon; neither approach would benefit those most likely to be interested in the search for best practices. We assume you will apply practical common sense when examining the steps and issues the book presents.

The material and methodology we examine are in no way limited to government agencies. They apply also to nonprofit organizations and public colleges and universities, which face challenges similar to those faced by governing bodies; all are bureaucracies perceived as slow to change, yet they are experiencing shrinking budgets and customer demands for more and better service.

Successfully benchmarking for best practices in the public sector requires a great deal more than mastering the technical process, of course. We do not want to give the impression that we have overlooked the unique realities of public sector operations. Let us acknowledge at this point some truths about working in the public arena; unless certain issues are dealt with up front, they may become serious obstacles. If the benchmarker's political constituencies are not lined up in support of the undertaking, for example, the project may never get off the ground. No public sector practitioner can separate the daily business of government from the political wheeling and dealing of its elected leaders, whose high rate of turnover has widespread impact. One day your champion is there; the next day she has been voted out of office. Other challenges in the public sector include a lack of people and money to conduct benchmarking activities. Planning for the limits of the budget and personnel before initiating a benchmarking project will contribute significantly to getting positive results.

The perceptions of politicians and unions create some of the major obstacles to benchmarking and implementing best practices. In Maryland, Governor Parris Glendening has installed community-oriented policing—a collaborative effort of the police and each neighborhood's residents and businesses to identify sources of crime and address community needs—as the centerpiece of his administration's crime policy. Glendening's most recent plans for a statewide police training facility were announced during a public ceremony where the keynote address was given by one of community policing's most ardent supporters, U.S. Attorney General Janet Reno. The ceremony gave the governor an opportunity to gain major political mileage by demonstrating to voters how committed he was to being tough on crime and how his efforts warranted the attention and praise of the nation's leading prosecutor. Coincidentally, the ceremony introducing the training facility took place just days after a police officer in Glendening's home county of Prince Georges publicly voiced strong doubt about administrators' support of and commitment to community policing (Jeter, 1995). The officer revealed to journalists his ongoing battle with his own department over his attempts to make the practice work. Here we have a politician, the governor, capitalizing on a best practice while the department heads responsible for its implementation may be sabotaging it from within. Bureaucratic infighting is one of the common side effects of trying to import a best practice from outside the home organization.

In order to succeed in Maryland, the practice of community-oriented policing will have to overcome a lack of acceptance within law enforcement agencies. The nonacceptance arises from the conflicts between the practice and the organizational culture into which it is imported. First, police departments follow a strict hierarchy; community policing challenges that hierarchy by empowering patrol officers to devise and implement their own solutions. Second, law enforcement officials distrust the method because it is an untested and unwelcome departure from the model that has been the standard for over fifty years. Third, long-held traditions are tough to change, especially in the face of the brotherhood of the police union. Officers who joined the force seeking danger and excitement understandably may be reluctant to accept their new, less glamorous role. Police officers are trained to arrest, not to counsel, and opponents have charged that the method turns police officers into social workers with guns. By signing up the Prince Georges police department as a sponsor of the new training facility, the governor may have dealt effectively with an entrenched bureaucracy that was not interested in breakthrough improvement. Time will tell. This scenario is not limited to public safety organizations; it can appear in any type of bureaucratic agency.

Just as competing interests of unions and the executive branch must be addressed, reinvention and reengineering efforts cannot ignore the existence and role of legislative bodies. One of the most powerful criticisms of the Gore Report (National Performance Review, 1993) is that it did not address the role of Congress in creating and changing executive branch structure and operations. At the federal level, it is Congress that ultimately determines an agency's purpose and goals. NPR ignored the level of cooperation from Congress needed to carry out its recommendations.

Ronald Moe (1995) highlighted the offices of the inspectors general as an example of NPR naïveté. Under the section "Cutting Red Tape," Vice President Gore has a worthy goal: to stop holding civil servants accountable for the process and start holding them accountable for results. The goal is followed by a six-part action plan to bring it to fruition. Step four in this plan calls for the reorientation of the inspectors general, "to shift their focus from punishing those who violate rules and regulations to helping agencies learn to perform better" (National Performance Review, 1993, p. 13). As admirable as that goal is, the adversarial position of the inspectors general was part of their original mandate. Moe's point is that in order to change the mandate, Congress must first change the law.

In their project designs, organizations searching for best practices need to address the cooperation required from legislative bodies; they should make sure that benchmarking and efforts to institute best practices have the support, not the antagonism, of the legislators who represent the people.

A major challenge for any organization undergoing preparation for benchmarking is the identification of potential barriers. Background research and briefings from agency officials should reveal regulatory requirements that may come into conflict with imported practices. Government agencies at all levels operate under statutory requirements that their private sector counterparts do not have to deal with. Regulations do not have to prevent the use of best practices, but they do add another degree of difficulty. For example, a 1995 GAO report reveals that Department of Defense officials were concerned that using private sector distributors to deliver food to dining facilities on military bases would eliminate the participation of small businesses. Their concern was alleviated when the GAO discovered that most of the preexisting private sector distributors were in fact small businesses (General Accounting Office, May 1995). In this situation, regulations did not conflict with the performance improvement efforts of the Department of Defense; however, other agencies may not always be so fortunate.

Public sector benchmarking is a practice in its infancy, and cases have been scarce. To illustrate aspects of the methodology, we have found it necessary to refer repeatedly to several cases that are well documented. Readers should keep in mind that the sample is small and the number of efforts with demonstrable results is even smaller.

Throughout the book, we have illustrated as many concepts as possible using two case studies with which we are personally familiar: a joint benchmarking study conducted by Salt Lake City and Reno on customer service; and a three-part benchmarking study, drawn from West Virginia's Inspire Initiative, on employee training, customer satisfaction, and one-stop business registration. We refer to these cases frequently as we bring to life the elements of the benchmarking process.

Benchmarking and the search for best practices is a powerful and promising new tool for the public sector and public administrators. This book will make the analysis, testing, and adoption of best practices easier for politically sensitive public environments.

Part One

Preparing for Benchmarking

| Understanding Best Practices

Defining a best practice is reminiscent of attempts at defining equity, pornography, or program outcomes: much has been written, but little has been agreed on. Nevertheless there are three common ways of defining best practices.

1. *A best practice is anything better than your current practice.* Practitioners today are strongly connected to each other through professional relationships and professional associations, in the United States and internationally, and they all seem to be looking for ways to improve. They speak excitedly about new ways of doing business outside their home organization and seem willing to consider any practice that may help their own organizations to improve. When John Scully at NAPA set up a database that included the best practices report published by the U.S. Conference of Mayors, he received over two hundred inquiries about the report within the first seven days.

We have encountered enthusiasm about efforts to improve in many conversations with government officials. Gene Davis, of the Department of Management and Finance in Arlington County, Virginia, told us about fire chiefs in Reno, Nevada, who were working to uncover the best practices for keeping firefighters busy when there are no fires. Mitchel Glassman of the Federal Deposit Insurance Corporation (FDIC) reported that the United States is assisting the new Republic of Slovenia to establish a Bank Rehabilitation Agency.

When practitioners learn about new ideas or practices, they frequently refer to these discoveries as best practices, probably because of the popularity of this term and because it suggests that there really is a "best" way of doing things in an organization. But as we shall see, the term is relative, and its meaning can depend on the speaker who has discovered a best practice and the organization to which he or she belongs.

This relativistic approach to best practices has some dangers. For example, in *Reinventing Government,* David Osborne and Ted Gaebler (1992) wrote that a parks and recreation employee with the city of Visalia, California, arranged to have a municipal swimming pool financed on relatively short notice—a potential best practice. However, the rush to install the pool resulted in soil excavation problems, cost overruns, and political fights. Visalia overlooked important aspects of the initiative, and the citizens lost faith in their managers and elected officials.

Another example of a city that had to reassess its approach is Phoenix, Arizona, widely recognized for successfully introducing competition into its collection of solid waste. Some divisions within the Phoenix Department of Sanitation were able to collect waste at costs comparable to or better than those of private firms; some divisions could not compete and lost their portion of the city's business to private firms. Other cities followed Phoenix's lead, enthralled that government could perform as well as private industry (even though portions of Phoenix's services were lost to the private sector). We later discovered some problems with privatizing this function, however. One is that cities sell or lose equipment as part of the privatization transition. If they later decide to retake the service, as Phoenix did, they end up making large capital outlays. Although privatizing solid waste appeared at first to be a best practice, it did not have a sufficient life cycle to prove itself.

Still others consider a best practice to be any emerging industry trend that seems to make sense. For example, the Gore Report (National Performance Review, 1993) recommends that a variety of what it refers to as best practices be adopted by the federal government; they include high-speed networks, electronic benefits transfer, and public access to on-line data. These are all good ideas, but are they really best practices?

This first definition of a best practice is too global and less than helpful for practitioners trying to understand how to adapt a practice to their home organization. Using a relativistic definition of best practice can put an organization in the risky position of importing ideas, not practices, that ultimately may cause more harm than good. The risk is that too many unproven ideas will be tried and that precious dollars will be wasted in areas that produce minimal fiscal returns.

2. *A best practice is declared by the media or others.* Periodicals such as *Governing* and *Public Management,* which run articles on current methodologies such as reengineering, quality management, information mapping, or benchmarking, showcase the successes enjoyed by their practitioner audiences. They tend to view a best practice as some action or activity that helped an organization to overcome an obstacle. Unfortunately these periodicals are not in agreement on terms and are not consistent when writing about best practices.

Numerous books have touted best practices as well. *Reinventing Government* is filled with innovative practices held out as examples. David Carr and Ian Littman's *Excellence in Government* (1990) describes how many federal, state, and local governments developed outstanding practices by using quality management and focusing on customer service. In *Reinventing Government,* the need for sustained and proven success takes a back seat to the drama and impact of unique and innovative practices.

In some instances a best practice is published by the organization that uses the practice or even individuals or groups that have some familiarity with the topic. In 1994 the U.S. Conference of Mayors, wanting to recognize excellence in government, sought the best and brightest ideas from numerous cities, which it then compiled into a document of best practices. The criteria? The solicitation simply asked, "What seems to be working well in your city?" The result is a compilation of various cities' most prized programs and activities. Although the report is an interesting compendium, it is not a collection of best practices; a large number of the practices have little, if any, empirical evidence of having yielded tangible results. The lack of tangible results is understandable in many circumstances, but not when an activity is touted as a best practice.

In West Virginia a Measuring Customer Satisfaction benchmarking team identified certain gaps between its agency—the Division of Motor Vehicles—and the private sector. The research showed, for instance, that every one of the private sector agencies the team queried uses and validates surveys, but only 58 percent of state government agencies use surveys, and only 35 percent actually validate them. This research indicated a discrepancy but not necessarily a best practice. Surveys are a tool that can help reveal best practices; they are not best practices in and of themselves.

In another instance the Department of Veterans Affairs (VA) hired a consulting firm to compile a list of best practices. The firm interviewed industry experts on what they saw as a best practice, but the criteria seemed to be solely the wisdom and good judgment of experienced people. We do not mean to disparage these industry experts, but quantifiable data often prove gut instincts wrong. And it seems the VA spent more funds on compiling the list of practices than preparing itself to import the practices and change.

Some organizations have been independently encouraging the search for best practices and benchmarking. The International Benchmarking Clearinghouse of the American Productivity and Quality Center (APQC) systematically constructed a database of best practices. In this database a best practice is a factual abstract describing organizations with successful or innovative practices in numerous business processes. The database pulls together selective items from the vast ocean of information available for benchmarking research. The question for practitioners who might use this database is, How would I know which declared best practice is right for my home agency or organization? Considering the volumes of information available, this is a daunting question.

It is important to remember that a best practice is not a fixed way of doing things but something that changes over time and from one organization to another. When officials in Salt Lake City asked the iKon Group to benchmark cities for effective customer inquiries and complaints processes, we discovered just how a best practice can change shape. Seattle may have been the source for such a process; Charlotte, North Carolina, then modeled its process on Seattle's; Arlington County, Virginia, modified the Charlotte model; and now Salt Lake City may make further changes. Best practices multiply so fast that we cannot track them all. Some have positive effects after they are modified; others may not.

Several organizations have attempted to put together lists of best practices. Revenue Canada, the Canadian tax collection agency, has developed the EXCELLENCE database of over seven hundred exemplary practices, which it shares through electronic bulletin boards. Revenue Canada has found the board to be a gold mine of practical information that contributes to improved services, participative leadership, team building, and communication skills (Lawrence, 1994, p. 22).

Unfortunately the bulletin boards seem to be a free-for-all system with no manager, priorities, or ranking of practices. How much more useful it might have been if Revenue Canada had carefully selected the vital few successes for systematic dissemination. Has the cost of establishing and maintaining the database yielded tangible, measurable results? In the excitement and enthusiasm for best practices, practitioners sometimes neglect to take a thoughtful, systematic approach to data collection.

In another effort to compile best practices, NAPA's Alliance for Redesigning Government established the Public Innovator's Information Cooperative. This database, broken down into seven topics, includes case studies from numerous governments in a variety of policy fields and functions. It is somewhat unwieldy, however, with hundreds of entries and tips.

Revenue Canada and NAPA should be commended for their ability to organize and make readily available this important information. We must recognize, however, that in the search for best practices, these ad hoc sources are only the tip of the iceberg. A considerable amount of thought and energy should be devoted to finding the most salient and appropriate best practice for each organization.

3. *A best practice is an award-winning success.* Perhaps the most reliable definitions of best practices arise from the numerous award and recognition programs throughout the United States. The President's Award and the President's Prototype Award have yielded dozens of examples of successful practices, mostly in the federal sector.

Another example is the Carl Bertelsmann Prize for the best-managed city. In 1993 the competition was based on performance in customer service, employee involvement, planning, innovation, and bureaucratic downsizing (Kwok, 1993, p. A9). The prize recognizes municipalities that have innovatively adjusted their structure and operations to meet challenges and have overcome their traditional authority model. The award also is designed to encourage other cities to begin their own transformation ("Performance and Democracy," n.d., p. 11).

Rutgers University's Exemplary State and Local Awards Program (EXSL) has recognized over one hundred jurisdictions and organizations for outstanding performance. The award criteria are set out in a report by the National Center for Public Productivity (1995, n.p.):

- A program's direct impact on problem addressed
- A program's impact on delivery of services
- A program's effectiveness, costs, and benefits
- Client satisfaction
- A program's ability to be adopted elsewhere
- Innovative nature of the program
- Overall program rating

In some cases agencies themselves identify what they consider their award-winning programs. When Barrett and Greene (1993) were preparing their study of pace-setting cities, they asked selected cities to tell them which of their programs worked well. They then had people in national organizations that specialized in selected topic areas help them identify the best program in each area. The reviewers made some interesting determinations. For example, it was decided that San Francisco had excelled in developing AIDS programs, but Seattle had made significant improvements on the San Francisco model, so awards went to both.

Some agencies have made internal best practices awards. The General Services Administration instituted an individual award for best practices, which has gone to, among others, a computer scientist at the U.S. Geological Survey for promoting the use of CD-ROM for disseminating and storing large amounts of data. The Air Force Standard Systems Center has given awards for the following best practices: substantial user involvement in systems development, with one-third of the staff drawn from user disciplines such as supply and aircraft maintenance; the rigorous use of software engineering disciplines (including the software maturity model from the Software Engineering Institute at Carnegie-Mellon University); and a twenty-four-hour, sixty-person help desk that handles twelve thousand calls per month (Anthes, 1994, p. 16).

Needed: A Better Definition of Best Practice

Clearly the research on best practices has been imprecise, loosely defined, and broadly focused. And there is very little, if any, evidence that these practices have been transported with success (Overman and Boyd, 1994). What evidence that does exist is ad hoc and random.

Make no mistake, we strongly believe that thousands of public organizations have benefited by importing practices discovered from other organizations. The problem is that the academic and practitioner communities have failed to articulate an adequate definition of best practices and to understand how various practices have successfully been imported. The phrase *best practices* has reached a high level of use yet has such limited clarity that it warrants attention. *Best practices* does not mean simply making comparisons and sharing practices. We must continue to grow in applying a systematic method to finding best practices. Finding a best practice has a specific form and use. Establishing criteria is the first step toward outlining what a best practice is.

Best Practices Criteria

We have developed criteria for defining a best practice based on a variety of sources (and we expect the criteria to be refined as research and practice evolve). We examined hundreds of accepted examples of best practices in periodicals such as *Governing, Public Management,* and *Public Productivity and Management Review* and tried to tease out common themes from these proven successes. In our search we found a number of descriptors—for example, "performance that steadily climbs over time until there is dramatic breakthrough or large percentage gain" (National Performance Review, 1995, p. 6) and "management practices that high-performing organizations use to align and continuously improve business processes and infrastructure to support strategic market objectives" (Coopers & Lybrand, n.d., p. 2).

Finally, we added some aspects of quality management and common sense to our criteria. The search for a best practice should address an activity that is resource intensive and has a significant impact on external customers. We came up with seven criteria for defining best practices:

Best Practices Criteria

1. *Successful over time.* A best practice must have a proven track record.
2. *Quantifiable results.* The success of a best practice must be quantifiable.
3. *Innovative.* A program or practice should be recognized by its peers as being creative or innovative.
4. *Recognized positive outcome.* If quantifiable results are limited, a best practice may be recognized through other positive indicators.
5. *Repeatable.* A best practice should be replicable with modifications. It should establish a clear road map, describing how the practice evolved and what benefits are likely to accrue to others who adopt the practice.
6. *Has local importance.* Best practices are salient to the organization searching for improvement. The topic, program, process, or issue does not need to be identical to the importing organization, however.
7. *Not linked to unique demographics.* A best practice may have evolved as a result of unique demographics, but it should be transferable, with modifications, to organizations where those demographics do not necessarily exist.

It is frequently said that public management is as much an art as a science. Our criteria, which we will now examine in greater detail, represent the empirical aspect of the search for best practices; applying the criteria is more of an artistic endeavor.

1. Successful over Time

A best practice must have a track record. Although results may come instantly with some practices, especially when technology is introduced, a minimum of a six-month track record should exist. Because some practices take longer to get results, two years may be required to reveal a best practice. Although this may seem like an inordinate period of time, it is merely two data points for seasonal processes such as snow removal or annual tax processing. And although an organization may declare a best practice at two years, a three-to-five-year trend may be required for more conservative organizations to be convinced that they should consider the practice.

Some critics may view the data trend criterion as burdensome. After all, an organization experiencing a crisis must act quickly and cannot wait two years for an answer. We agree that in many instances an organization will not have the luxury of researching and implementing best practices. In these cases we consider the organization to be pursuing *better* practices. Nevertheless we strongly suggest that a practice without a reliable history of success may not be a best practice; in fact, it may not be successful and may go entirely in the wrong direction.

We do not want to discourage public organizations from continually seeking ideas from colleagues, peers, and publications. However, when there is a special need or desire to focus on a specific area or if precision is important, you must use reliable criteria to select and adapt the practice to your home organization.

2. Quantifiable Results

The success of a best practice should be quantifiable. Too often, in their zeal to respond to political and fiscal pressures, organizations are willing to try anything for a quick fix. Sometimes, though, that quick fix can make the situation far worse. The U.S. Internal Revenue Service carefully tested its electronic filing program—collecting data on the number of returns filed, the error rates, costs, and satisfaction of users such as H & R Block—before declaring it a best practice for others to adopt. The success of a practice is conveyed through output, outcome, timeliness, error rates, efficiency, or effectiveness measures. A single data point does not necessarily mean success.

On the other hand we must guard against overdependency on the use of measures to identify best practices. In our work we have come across comparative data that suggest one organization is performing significantly better than another, but with additional investigation, we discovered that the data were unreliable or had been misinterpreted. "Quantifiable results" is only one criterion that points to a best practice.

3. Innovative

A program or practice should be recognized as creative or innovative by its people in the field. The challenge is to determine what is innovative and what is merely an incremental change in existing practices. The practice should represent a substantial deviation from the norm. Many pilot initiatives have the makings of a best practice; others are merely excuses for trying something that we all know works but needs some political support. For example, the Arlington County, Virginia, Department of Zoning plans to shift front-desk personnel to assist with the more complex tasks in the back office area, and vice versa, depending on the workload. Shifting staff to match the workload is a good management practice that may represent incremental improvement on the current process. Measurable results, however, do not automatically confer best practice status.

4. Recognized Positive Outcome

If there is a positive outcome but quantifiable results are limited, a best practice may be recognized through other indicators. For example, Seattle established satellite offices to serve constituents. These offices provide direct services and act as organizing units for community events. Salt Lake City and Reno representatives visited some of these offices and formed a favorable impression of them; however, quantifiable measures of the satellites' success were limited. The indicators must be generally accepted by peers as meaningful and reliable information about results.

5. Repeatable

A best practice should be replicable with modifications. It should establish a clear road map, describing how the practice evolved and what the benefits to others who adopt the practice are likely to be. Ideally a best practice is one that has already been adapted in other subdivisions of the originating organization.

6. Has Local Importance

Best practices are salient to the organization searching for improvement, although the process does not have to be identical to that of the organization seeking improvement. One challenge public organizations face is overcoming the not-invented-here syndrome. Importing a best practice can fail because some implementers see the initiative as having local importance, and others believe their organization is unique, so the practice will not work.

7. Not Linked to Unique Demographics

A best practice may have evolved as a result of unique demographics, but it should be transferable, with modifications, to organizations where those demographics do not necessarily exist. Magnet schools, for example, grew from unique circumstances, but the practices used in those schools can be applied to virtually any school system.

We recognize that applying these criteria will reduce the number of examples of best practices, but those that remain will be important ones. When we applied the criteria to the compilation of best practices by the U.S. Conference of Mayors, fewer than 10 of 162 practices met the criteria. Our goal is not to disparage the successes described in the Conference report but rather to focus clearly on the vital few that justify consideration for importing to our own cities or other public entities.

We also recognize that identifying the best practice is only half of the problem. The other half is importing and implementing the new practice. The American Institute of Certified Public Accountants (AICPA) and the Hackett Group (1994) jointly sponsored a study of financial companies. Their baseline analysis of costs and efficiencies for finance and accounting functions included twenty-seven processes. Although their goal was to help finance and accounting departments to improve by adopting best practices, participants in the study received only comparative reports. The participants had to choose their own partners and analyze their internal processes with little, if any, assistance. Only half the problem was solved.

Best Practices or Better Practices?

We do not want to leave the impression that a search for best practices has to be as prolonged or difficult as the search for the Holy Grail. Many large and small public organizations do not have the funds or staff resources to support an extensive search. Similarly the political environment may not tolerate a search for the best. And even if a search for the best is possible, once that practice is found, it may be impossible to import it because of the organization's lack of readiness. For these and a host of other reasons, we recognize that many public organizations must limit their search to finding a better practice than their current one. Regardless, we caution against the relativistic approach we have described and encourage paying attention to two dimensions: the simplicity of the process itself and the similarity of the organization, or partner, with which a performance comparison is being made. (We expand on these two dimensions in Chapters Two and Three.) Each dimension, and therefore the search for a better or best practice, becomes more complex as the process becomes more complex and the partner selected is increasingly different. We urge organizations looking for a better practice to limit their scope, beginning with simple processes or possibly comparing themselves to similar organizations. They must be sure to hone their methodology, paying close attention to the steps of importing and sustaining the practice. As their skills develop and they have success, practitioners can become more adventurous in searching for breakthrough solutions. (The initial benchmarking study does not have to take place within the organization.)

Best Practices and Performance Measures

Two fundamental questions should precede the search for a best practice: How do we know how well our agency or organization is doing? Is our performance improving or deteriorating? Only then should these questions be followed by this third question: Who is doing something better than us? Although meaningful answers to the first two questions are essential to improving performance, in fact, the search for a best practice sometimes precedes an understanding of the organization's current performance. We find that sequence problematic.

Performance measurement, as it has come to be understood in the public sector, is the process of quantifying—or assigning a number to—the operation of a process, program, or any other activity through which a public agency delivers products or services to its customers. For example, fire departments measure the operation of their activities by measuring response time (the amount of time it takes firefighters to arrive at a site after a call for assistance has been received), the number of fire inspections conducted, the number of code violations corrected, and a multitude of other indicators that reflect how well the departments are providing service to their customers.

Developing good performance measures is not an easy task. For example, how does one identify and define the set of rules for assigning a number to the activity "driving safely"? Is it the number of accidents a driver is involved in? What about drivers who put in twice as many miles as some other drivers? Is a better measure the number of accidents per thousand miles driven? The number of tickets received? But would the latter standard be prejudicial to drivers in urban locales, who face more traffic congestion than drivers in rural areas?

So how does an agency develop performance measures? Some agencies already have measures of their programs' effectiveness (how well they accomplish what they are supposed to be doing) or efficiency (at what cost they accomplish what they are doing). If your agency has no measures, you need to go back to its reason for existing. What are its mission, program, and services? Who are its customers? What do customers expect from the agency? What are the agency's goals and objectives? How will you know whether the agency is achieving its mission, goals, and objectives?

The performance measures selected vary dramatically, depending on the mission of the agency (department, division, program, service, and so forth). For instance, a procurement department we were working with defined its mission as "awarding contracts that, when protested by the nonselected vendors, are never overturned by the appeals board." Its measure of performance was the number of contracts awarded without being overturned during the appeal process. Not surprisingly its customers defined its mission somewhat differently: "delivering the needed resources at the right time at the least cost to the government." The customers' preferred performance measure was the percentage of time their resource needs were met on time through the procurement process. With two such radically different concepts of what the mission of the procurement organization should be, the difficulty of developing performance measures that accurately reflect the operation of the procurement function is clear.

Thus a critical step in developing performance measures is to get the agency and its key stakeholders to agree on what the mission of the agency is, what goals and objectives need to be established and achieved to accomplish that mission, and what essential measures can serve as indicators of performance in the delivery of the mission. These measures are the vital few that need to be identified to determine what the agency is accomplishing. The baggage handling division of a city airport may have performance measures such as the amount of time it takes to get a bag from the aircraft to the baggage claim area, the number of bags lost or misplaced, and the number of passenger complaints per thousand passengers passing through the airport. A revenue collection agency might measure the dollars collected, the number of audits, the delinquent revenues, and the number of litigations.

No single performance measure (or even an individual process, program, or service) is likely to reflect the operation of an agency accurately. Thus agencies need to develop a group of measures to account for overall performance, and together these measures should give an accurate picture of what the agency does. Note that these performance measures do not by themselves give an indication of how the agency does what it does or how well it does it. Performance measures take a snapshot of an agency at a point in time. They are descriptive of what the agency is doing. Performance measurement collects data in order to understand how the agency produced the products and services reflected in the measures, to gain some insight into how well the agency is performing, and to figure out what needs improving. Thus performance measures can identify what to benchmark in the effort to improve.

Many public sector organizations have not developed performance measures to the extent desired. Can the departments or divisions that lack sophisticated performance measurement systems conduct an effective benchmarking study and search for the best practice? A benchmarking purist may unequivocally say no, but our answer is yes—with a few caveats.

If even a few or limited measurements exist, they should be applied to the methodology described in subsequent chapters. At a minimum there must be measures that reliably point to areas that are resource intensive or problematic. How else will you know that you are searching for worthy improvements?

Typically, high-cost areas are ripe for improvement. Areas with a large number of complaints also have great potential, though the mere fact that they receive many complaints does not necessarily mean they are good candidates for benchmarking. For example, the IRS receives numerous complaints about tax collection actions. This results from resistance to paying taxes, not from the IRS process itself. The agency would not be wise to invest a significant amount of resources in benchmarking the complaints, but could benefit from benchmarking the collection process—for example, with credit card companies—to improve efficiency and timeliness.

When virtually no measures exist, it may be important to establish baseline data before embarking on the benchmarking study. Salt Lake City and Reno jointly collected performance data before looking outside for best practices in the customer referral process. A thirty-day data collection period revealed some surprises about the source of customer calls and helped the benchmarkers develop more salient questions for the site visits to Charlotte and Seattle; these visits helped them better understand what they needed to measure. Thus, embarking on a benchmarking study before sophisticated measures were in place ultimately helped them to determine which measures to install.

Quality Management and the Search for Best Practices

Quality management, embraced by public and private organizations across the country, offers a worthy framework for understanding why we must search for best practices. Originally implemented in Japan, quality management was initially adopted by the private sector in the United States. As with many other management practices, the public sector began to consider and use quality management several years after private sector companies obtained proven results. The public entities that have adopted quality management with significant empirical results include the Department of Defense, the Department of Energy, the Internal Revenue Service, the states of Arkansas and Florida, and the cities of Madison, Wisconsin, and Salt Lake City, Utah.

Although the details vary from author to author, there are some essential elements of quality management (see Figure 1.1):

- Top-level commitment to change
- Passion for identifying, meeting, and exceeding customer requirements
- Continuous feedback and improvement
- Empowering employees and teams to improve
- Measuring processes and performance
- Strategic or long-term focus

A quality management approach means that resources are dedicated to improving customer service, finding ways to improve processes, and empowering employees to make decisions. Quality management cannot be achieved quickly, and many organizations select a multiyear, systematic approach, implementing some basic steps and tools first and then proceeding to more sophisticated steps, tools, and techniques.

Two components of quality management are especially important to benchmarking and finding best practices: measuring processes and performance, and continuous feedback and improvement. Measurements answer the question, How are we performing? Continuous feedback and improvement answer the question, What can we do to get better? West Virginia's Inspire Initiative, which serves as one of our case studies, was launched by Governor Gaston Caperton as a four-part program—empowerment, benchmarking, performance measures, and performance-based budgeting—that reflects a quality management approach.

Figure 1.1. Components of Quality Management.

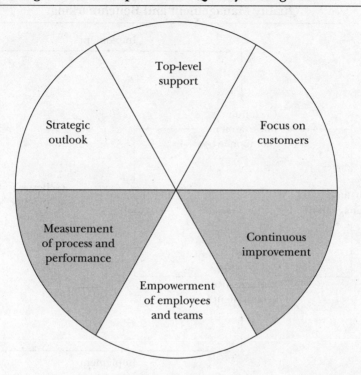

Measuring, so important to quality management, relies on benchmarking as a tool (see Figure 1.2). How do you know what to improve unless you have some measure that tells you about a performance problem? Once the problem has been defined and then measured, tools are selected to help find improvement opportunities. Among the tools available to identify where and how to improve continuously are customer surveys and benchmarking. Benchmarking, whether conducted internally or externally, reveals the best practice that, if implemented correctly, will significantly improve performance.

For several years the private sector has used benchmarking—considered one of the more advanced quality management tools—as one of several ways to find improvement opportunities. The public sector is only now beginning to grasp the complexity

Figure 1.2. Relationships Between
Quality Management and Benchmarking.

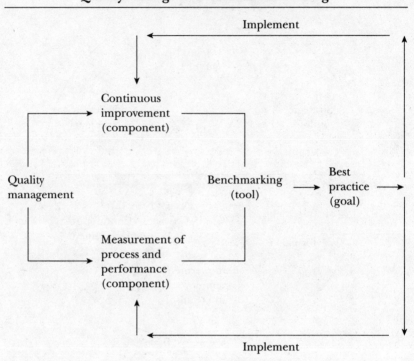

and power of benchmarking, which has as its outcome one or more best practices. The practice is implemented, and the cycle begins again. Measurements indicate the degree of success, tools are applied to areas that need improvement, and so on.

Although our model may appear simple, the realities of day-to-day government operations make implementation tough. The remaining chapters of this book focus on how to make the challenges less difficult.

Chapter Two

Benchmarking to Identify Best Practices

Benchmarking has been predominantly a private sector activity. Businesses were quick to grasp that benchmarking produces more bang for the buck in their process improvement efforts and allows them to work smarter while cutting costs; it is simply a better and cheaper way to improve business practices. The private sector has had remarkable success with benchmarking for best practices. General Electric cut costs and improved customer service by benchmarking Ford. To improve its printed wiring board assembly process and coolant management, Texas Instruments (TI) studied industry leaders in each process. Winner of the Baldrige award in 1992, TI has produced continuous process improvement and achieved world-class performance. After witnessing the possibilities of benchmarking, other corporations have raced to jump on the benchmarking bandwagon and reap the benefits of the new tool.

The Ritz-Carlton hotel chain, another 1992 Baldrige winner, benchmarked a competitor to increase efficiency and reduce the cycle time of its room cleaning process. Ritz-Carlton management found that cleaning teams working nonconsecutively in accordance with front desk requirements are far more efficient than individual cleaners going room to room. Unlike individuals, the teams were able to avoid retracing or repeating steps and to prepare rooms according to the specific needs of the front desk. After benchmarking the process, the Ritz-Carlton implemented this best practice in one site. The results were overwhelming: a decrease in costs from the previous year of almost $100,000 and a rise in employee satisfaction of 13.6 percent. The chain then used this facility to demonstrate the new practices, teach representatives from other sites, and develop a program for implementation throughout the company (International Institute for Learning, 1995a, p. 24). Corporations that have adopted best practices understand that benchmarking is a rapid way of achieving improvement because it relies on breakthrough thinking and does not require inventing new solutions.

Private industry has also capitalized on the strengths of government agencies in benchmarking efforts. For example, the AICPA and the Hackett Group, a Cleveland-based consulting firm, constructed for the use of certified public accountants a database containing extensive information on key management practices of more than fifty major corporations and government entities ("News Report," 1993, p. 15). Government agencies have been collecting data and making comparisons for years but seldom take the next step: identifying the top performers and importing best practices. Today, benchmarking is the most sensible route for public sector agencies seeking to improve performance. Government managers need to emulate their private sector counterparts in the practice of benchmarking and begin to import best practices from other organizations.

Officials in Dallas, Texas, have created an excellent example of what can happen when a locality adopts benchmarking. Dallas administrators vigilantly monitor the number of police per square mile, spending per capita, and percentage of crimes solved and then compare those numbers with nine other major cities. Barrett and Greene (1993) have noted that Dallas has "few peers in the use of measurement" (p. 42), just one of the reasons that Dallas was named best-run city in the United States by *Financial World* in 1993. The municipal government understands that it must constantly ask why another jurisdiction is operating better or with lower costs. Keep reminding your organization that reinventing is a waste of precious resources.

What Is Benchmarking?

In our attempt to construct a working definition of benchmarking, we surveyed the literature. A quick analysis boiled down the reigning views of benchmarking to the most common characteristics associated with it:

- Four definitions include comparison or comparing.
- Two definitions mention practices.
- Six refer to performance.
- Four include the words *outstanding, best,* or *leaders.*
- Three refer to improvement.
- Three call benchmarking a process, and three apply it to processes.
- Three say it includes measuring.

From this analysis we can see that benchmarking is most commonly known as a process of measuring and comparing to identify ways to improve processes and achieve higher performance. This formulaic definition is somewhat awkward, so for the purposes of this book, we will use the following definition: *Benchmarking is a process for identifying and importing best practices to improve performance.*

Thus benchmarking is a process—a series of actions, steps, functions, or activities that bring about an end or a result: the identification and importation of best practices to improve performance. Note that simply identifying best practices—that is, without importing them to your own organization—is not benchmarking. Nor is importing practices that have not been identified as best or most effective. To ensure that the process both identifies and imports best practices, benchmarking uses a methodology: a series of steps or actions that will lead to discovering best practices, help to adapt the practice to a particular organization, and facilitate the adoption of the best practice to improve performance. (The methodology is presented briefly in this chapter and is covered in detail in Chapter Five.)

There are other definitions of benchmarking. Richard J. Fischer (1994) defines benchmarking as "comparing the performance of your agency with that of others with outstanding performance to find fresh approaches and new ideas" (p. S2). Kenneth Bruder and Edward Gray (1994) seem to agree with Fischer; they view benchmarking as "a rigorous yet practical process for measuring your organization's performance and processes against those of best-in-class organizations, both public and private, and then using this analysis to improve services, operations, and costs dramatically" (p. S9). According to the APQC, benchmarking is "the process of continuously comparing and measuring an organization against business leaders anywhere in the world to gain information that will help an organization improve its performance" (Weisendanger, 1993, p. 20). AICPA/Hackett, in their ongoing financial process study, describe benchmarking as "the comparison of similar processes across organizations, companies, and industries to identify opportunities for improvement" (Hackett Group, 1994, p. 3914.2). In contrast, the Innovation Group specifically targeted "best in class" when they dubbed best practices benchmarking as "an investigation of why the best in class are in fact as good as they are" (n.d., p. 4).

For the Oregon Progress Board, benchmarking measures progress toward the particular vision and desired status of well-being for an agency, municipality, or community (Oregon Progress Board, 1994, p. 2). This meaning suggests an internal focus; the label of "best" is not circumscribed by another's performance but by the organization's vision of its future self. Not only is "best" not quantifiable in this definition, it is not even referred to.

Still another benchmarking authority, the International Institute for Learning (IIL) (1995a), depicted the process of searching for best practices as just one of the many critical reasons to benchmark. IIL has put forth two definitions of benchmarking; one is quite conventional, the other unique. The first is a practical operating definition: "The process of identifying, understanding, and adapting outstanding practices from organizations anywhere in the world to help your organization improve its performance" (p. 10). The second one reaches deeper into the psyche of an organization that will be successful at benchmarking others: "The practice of being humble enough to admit that someone else is better at something and wise enough to try and learn how to match and even surpass them at it" (p. 10).

We built our definition—that benchmarking is a process for identifying and importing best practices to improve performance—to include the key concepts of what makes benchmarking unique and distinguishable from other process improvement activities, and yet to keep it as inclusive as possible of all the activities and purposes one may encounter in the search for best practices. Based on our definition of best practices set out in Chapter One, note that benchmarking is a process for finding and implementing best practices—not just better practices. The primary objective of benchmarking, after all, is to improve an agency's performance, not to find the world's best process just for the fun of the search.

What Benchmarking Is Not

Although it is imperative to understand what benchmarking is in order to use it correctly, it also helps to understand what it is not.

Benchmarking is not just a simple comparative study. Weisendanger (1993) explains the method best when she says that benchmarking "not only defines what an organization produces but how it designs, manufactures, and markets its products or services. Rather than relying solely on comparisons with direct competitors, it uses data from other industries" (p. 20). The process does not begin with data collection, and it does not end with data analysis. Many agencies and localities are experts at compiling all kinds of data from other cities and states, but at the point at which cooperation between the organizations could be most productive, they disconnect and act alone. What sets benchmarking apart from comparative studies is the borrowing, adapting, and adopting of the methods of others, not just reviewing their outcome data.

Benchmarking is not simply copying practices from other organizations. It is a process for identifying best practices, adapting them, and then implementing the practice to improve performance. Copying practices from other organizations without analysis, understanding, and adaptation is as likely to hurt performance as it is to improve it. And even when the newly copied practice improves performance, it was probably found serendipitously through industrial tourism rather than through benchmarking.

Benchmarking is not performance assessment. Thousands of public entities have engaged in performance measurement programs with a variety of catchy names. This performance measurement or assessment, however, is just one element or step in the benchmarking exercise. It only lays the foundation of data on which an organization will act to improve a process.

Benchmarks are not static. In order to work, benchmarks should not remain the same from year to year; instead, they should incorporate knowledge gained, a mission revised, and structural changes made. Necessarily, as new criteria for success are being established, mission, goals, and objectives must change accordingly (Fischer, 1994, p. S6). Just as animals encountering a new or changing environment adapt to meet the new requirements for survival, so should public organizations adapt to meet new standards, new technology, and new, often lower, levels of funding. Over time these adaptations may turn into mutations, just as they do in nature. An organization that makes major adaptations in its first benchmarking and best practices project and then reuses the same benchmarks in the following year will find that this practice undermines successful change. Improvement is an ongoing, repetitive activity in which complacency has no part.

Benchmarking is neither an anecdotal form of comparative analysis nor industrial tourism. Process improvement should not be an excuse to visit other organizations. The site visit to a benchmarking partner is as far from the first step in a project as it is from the last, nor is it the main component of the benchmarking process.

What Is a Benchmark?

Understanding the process of benchmarking is not synonymous with understanding what is meant by the term *benchmark*. A benchmark is a standard of performance. The standard may be established by the organization as a goal or expected level of performance or for various other reasons. Benchmarks may also be established by looking outside the organization. For example, if Portland is experiencing one fire death per one hundred thousand residents, and our city is experiencing five, we may need to adopt Portland's rate as a new benchmark and find out how Portland is achieving that level of performance. *Benchmarking* is a process that helps agencies to find high performance levels (benchmarks) in other organizations and learn enough about how they are achieving those levels so the practice or process producing the performance can be applied in one's own agency.

William Gay (1992) has called benchmarking a *"Consumer Reports* for the public sector" (p. 2). Benchmarks, he says, provide citizen-consumers with accurate and reliable information with which they can set standards, make comparisons, and judge performances. They have become "important tools in state government for setting program and budget priorities and for seeking interagency cooperation on broad issues" *(Public Sector Network News,* 1994a, p. 7).

In *Oregon Shines* (Oregon Economic Development Department, 1989), which details Oregon's goals, the state Economic Development Department describes benchmarks as the individual measures or indicators of progress toward the goals that a jurisdiction has set out to achieve in its strategic vision. The Oregon Progress Board (1994) makes the analogy that benchmarks are indicators of a state's social, economic, and environmental well-being, just as blood pressure, cholesterol levels, and other such indicators are signs of a person's health.

The term *benchmark* is also used in different instances in reference to a turning point, a milestone, a stage, an event, and even a crisis, but it is most commonly known as a standard. In regard to benchmarking for best practices, many in the field would argue that the benchmark means the highest possible performance, referring either to the highest level of performance currently existing or a level of performance that has yet to be seen but is on the immediate horizon.

For our purposes, *benchmark* is the standard, or performance level, established or aspired to by the benchmarking agency. The National Performance Review report on telephone service contains several sample practices and benchmarks—for instance, one world-class telephone organization augments its workforce with part-time employees to ensure coverage during peak demand periods. This practice sustains low attrition rates of 3 to 7 percent (the benchmark) for frontline positions in best-in-business organizations (National Performance Review, 1995, p. 17).

Purposes of Benchmarking

In his benchmarking workshop for the International Association of Fire Chiefs in August 1992, consultant William Gay termed benchmarking a "surrogate for the competitive forces that push businesses to achieve higher levels of quality and productivity" (Gay, 1992,

p. 1). Public entities are not vying with each other for the lion's share of the market or even corporate survival, so a driving mechanism is conspicuously absent within government. Governing institutions have always been viewed as perpetual-motion devices, maintaining the same steady, reliable pace year after year. Citizens perceive government programs as immovable objects and the services they provide as entrenched and unchanging; further, they have come to rely on these services to an enormous degree. Now, however, they are witnessing the immovable object meeting the irresistible force of fiscal retrenchment. Services that once seemed permanently ensconced have been loosened, scaled back, or eliminated.

The public sector can use benchmarking not only to change the pace of an organization but to move it forward in time by quantum leaps—to allow it to cope with fundamental change, continue to meet citizen expectations, and avoid disenfranchising any community group. Through various awards and honors programs, local jurisdictions are now vying with each other for national and international renown. Those that do not keep up with the pace will suffer the consequences, and so will their citizenry.

Fischer (1994, p. S4) sets out three reasons for the public sector to benchmark:

1. "To determine the criteria that underlie performance." Without criteria there is no basis, no foundation, for making comparisons. Comparisons made without criteria will lack validity, as will performance improvement goals based on those comparisons.

2. "To identify problem areas within respective services." Benchmarking the lowest-rated services is only logical. Benchmarking a top-rated service will not move the entire agency forward and may leave second-rate services to atrophy even further. Conduct process triage to prioritize which services need immediate attention and which can wait until later.

3. "To improve the delivery of those services by importing best practices." Just knowing where you stand in comparison with others (and why that is the case) is a significant accomplishment in itself, but it is not enough. Precious money and time will be wasted if the new knowledge and insight are not acted on and used to bring improvement. Remember that benchmark data are time sensitive and will expire quickly.

In still another view, the Public Management Group states that the purpose of benchmarking is to identify variability in performance and reduce it by optimizing imported processes (Gay, 1992, p. 22). The Oregon Progress Board would add another purpose: to assess "the degree to which a jurisdiction is achieving its strategic goals" ("Governing for Results," 1994, p. 12). Neither of these two purposes focuses on benchmarking to improve performance. We are not saying that these approaches are not useful or appropriate; however, without focusing on improvement, benchmark teams sometimes lose their direction, and the project is not as successful as it could be. Any organization can use outcome measures to monitor its internal improvement quarter to quarter, but new horizons can be discovered only through new ideas.

Organizational Reactions to Benchmarking

Benchmarking is first and foremost a technical method, but as IIL notes with its second definition, benchmarking has another side effect: it makes an organization face facts about itself. It is an owning-up, maturing exercise. Benchmarking teams—whether composed of employees, external consultants, or a combination of both—should know and expect that there will be backlash from individuals and groups within the agency. The backlash can result from a real or perceived threat to an individual's job or to an entire division's existence—or simply from fear of the unknown. Competent organizations overcome these hurdles and learn from their experiences. Differing educational levels, fears, expectations, and understandings of the benchmarking process have all been cultural factors that have resulted in backlash and affected the implementation of best practices.

One of West Virginia's three benchmarking projects, Employee Training, met with the resistance that frequently arises in this area. When the first phase of the state's total quality management program (INSPIRE) was initiated, new quality management techniques were introduced that were radically different from the hierarchical, authoritarian approach to which many employees were accustomed. Employees feared that the governor was instituting benchmarking in order to camouflage his intention to downsize.

West Virginia agencies dealt with this skepticism by employing design teams, made up of employees within various agencies, to provide support and promote understanding of phase one, the empowerment process. Agency newsletters published success stories about the process that gave employees examples of the savings that can eventually occur in worker hours and dollars—through working smarter, not harder. In addition, a facilitator network was established to deal with the differences that existed in the ways facilitators functioned in various agencies.

While this approach was fairly successful, employee skepticism was heightened when the second phase, benchmarking, was introduced because it was viewed as a form of micromanaged performance evaluation to support plans to downsize and eliminate jobs. Although response to this team's baseline survey was 100 percent, cultural factors resulted in resistance that will probably have some negative impact on the implementation of an employee training strategic plan.

Carla O'Dell (International Institute for Learning, 1995, p. 29) has identified five common responses to benchmarking that teams should be prepared to deal with when they present results:

1. *Skepticism and distrust.* Colleagues receiving benchmarking results that they are not prepared to accept will immediately enter a state of denial.

2. *Shoot the messenger.* The team member or members making the presentation of the performance comparison with top-performing organizations will be shot down on revealing what appears to be low or poor performance by a work unit. The entire benchmarking effort may enter a crash-and-burn mode if the comparison data are not revived and accepted.

3. *Not invented here.* Some workers may discredit any method that has been proved effective if it was not designed in-house and tailored to their unique circumstances.

4. *But we're different.* Similar to the not-invented-here response, this reaction accuses the presenter of comparing apples and oranges. The underlying belief is, "That agency does not provide the same service we do, so any technique they have, no matter how outstanding, is irrelevant to this agency's situation."

5. *We'll look into it.* This response displays adequate appreciation to the team for all its hard work, but then the results are filed or thrown away by those in charge, never to be seen again.

There are two other common responses that should be added to this list:

1. *We cannot afford it.* Members of the audience remind the presentation team that the budget has already been stretched to the limit and that they are not willing to forgo any other function or project for the sake of benchmarking.
2. *We do not have time.* Like the budget, all available personnel are already spread too thin. Every precious second is dedicated to a task of greater value than benchmarking.

These reactions are by no means mutually exclusive. They may occur in overlapping stages, one succeeding another, or all at once. Before presenting their results, benchmarking teams may want to alert the audience members to these common responses and help them to understand their own reactions. For benchmarking projects to be successful, these attitudes have to be neutralized. Otherwise they will drown out the message contained in the results and possibly sabotage the entire project.

Benchmarking Methodology: An Overview

Benchmarking is a powerful tool for improving organizational performance, and like any other approach or methodology, its application needs to fit within and support the goals, objectives, vision, and strategic plan of the agency. Before starting a benchmarking project, or as part of the start-up activities, an agency needs to assess its current status and the future it plans to build. This information can be used to construct the organization framework within which the benchmarking effort will operate. To build the framework, the organization needs to address these questions:

What do we already know about our future?

What is our analysis of what we know?

What is our present status?

What is our desired future status?

How do we reach that future status?

What are our strengths and weaknesses, and how do they apply to
the previous question?

No agency can afford to be world-class in every aspect of its
operations. Every organization must strategically determine where
it wants to be world-class, which of its processes could be best in
industry, and what processes can get away with being good enough
to satisfy constituents and stakeholders. Agencies must also strategically decide where they want to improve, because no agency can
benchmark and improve every process. From a consideration of
these strategic issues, the agency can build a framework for performance and improvement, identifying the areas in which it wants
to be world-class, best in industry, and good enough and then
establish the path for bringing about the performance improvement needed to accomplish these goals.

Several Views of the Benchmarking Process

Once the framework for a benchmarking project is set up, the
organization can begin the actual process. Again, as we developed
concise step-by-step instructions, we encountered several samples
from those who had preceded us, and as with benchmarking definitions, they did not necessarily agree. Kenneth A. Bruder and
Edward M. Gray (1994, pp. S9–S14) provide the following seven-
step checklist for public sector benchmarking:

1. Determine which functional areas within the organization are
   in greatest need of benchmarking.
2. Identify key performance measures to track cost, quality, and
   efficiency for the functions selected.
3. Choose best-in-class organizations for each function. Best in
   class is defined as organizations that perform a certain function at the lowest cost or with the highest degree of quality or
   efficiency.
4. Measure the performance of the best-in-class companies for
   each benchmarked function.
5. Measure the organization's performance for each benchmark,
   and identify gaps between it and the best in class.
6. Specify actions and programs to close the gaps. The analysis

must be translated into specific action items and must be supported by upper management. Also, the right individuals must be involved. (See Chapter Six for a discussion of whom to involve.)

7. Implement the agenda and monitor results (recalibrate annually).

Interestingly, Bruder and Gray recommend measuring the performance of the chosen best-in-class organizations, the benchmarking partners, first. In West Virginia, for example, the Measuring Customer Satisfaction project team felt that it was difficult to come up with a process description of the best practice being benchmarked without first interviewing prospective partners (West Virginia used the term *partner* to refer to external organizations). The team saw an advantage in running both the internal (baseline) survey and the partner survey concurrently, to ensure that the surveys were measuring the same things. From this point it would be a simple process to identify gaps between the two.

We have found, however, that taking the pulse of your own organization first, and then that of your partners, may reveal functional weaknesses and strengths that could lead you to recast the choices from Bruder and Gray's first step. This was certainly the case in Salt Lake City and Reno. Because the teams were working in tandem, it was essential for each to identify its own processes first and arrive at some agreement on what the goals and measurements should be. The teams ended up eliminating Portland as a partner because its processes were too similar to their own. Without having a good understanding of how their own agencies worked, Salt Lake City and Reno would not have known what to look for in a partner.

Weisendanger's guidelines (1993, p. 20) simplify the benchmarking process even further, narrowing it to just four steps:

1. Understanding and analyzing your own processes and performance in a given area
2. Looking at other departments within your company and other companies to see who excels at these processes
3. Collecting and sharing information through surveys, site visits, and consultants
4. Analyzing the data to see what portions of others' methods might work for you

Unlike Bruder and Gray's checklist, Weisendanger's list includes the know-thyself step (step one). Actually, although this step is not made explicit, it is embedded in Bruder and Gray's initial determination of which functions need the most attention. Note that Weisendanger's second step does not specify best in class and instead recommends locating companies or internal divisions that excel. Also, in step four, Weisendanger combines what others call the gap analysis with the actual importation of chosen methods. These are, in fact, two distinct stages. First, data are analyzed; then methods are chosen that will improve organization performance.

In another approach, Pacific Bell (Cartwright, 1995, n.p.) uses the following six simple steps:

1. Determine purpose and scope of project.
2. Select partners.
3. Document your own processes and performance.
4. Document partner's processes and performance.
5. Identify gaps.
6. Develop and implement action plans.

Pacific Bell begins with the most basic step, which will help define the depth, breadth, and overall size of the project. There will be fewer hurdles and misunderstandings if everyone on the benchmarking team is operating with the same set of parameters and assumptions. Bruder and Gray's first step is similar but not as comprehensive. "Determining purpose and scope" would include their first step (choosing functional areas that will benefit most from benchmarking) as a substep. At step two, Pacific Bell, like Weisendanger, forgoes designating the best in class as partners to select. As Weisendanger does, Pacific Bell also recommends that the benchmarker conduct a self-assessment before all partner assessments. Unlike most other benchmarking instruction sets, however, Pacific Bell's process ends with developing and implementing action plans, leaving out the steps of monitoring results and recalibrating benchmarks. Also, step six is unclear in that it does not reveal the purpose for developing and implementing action plans (which is to close the gaps identified in step five).

In an information sheet, "Benchmarking: A Method for Achieving Superior Performance in Fire and Emergency Medical

Services," the Public Management Group (PMG) (Gay, 1992, p.11) sets out ten steps for benchmarking:

1. Identify benchmarks.
2. Identify comparables.
3. Collect data.
4. Determine performance gap.
5. Communicate findings.
6. Establish improvement goals.
7. Develop action plan.
8. Implement actions.
9. Monitor results.
10. Recalibrate benchmarks.

In step one, benchmarkers are asked to identify benchmarks, not functions or processes that need rejuvenation. The "comparables" of step two refer to shared performance measures that will allow for apples-to-apples comparison among benchmarking partners. In step three, PMG has eliminated the quandary about which data a benchmarker should collect first—in-house data or those of a partner—by collapsing this process into one easy but vague step. Possibly the intent is for both sets of data to be collected simultaneously. Joining Pacific Bell and Weisendanger, PMG does not specifically call for the collection of data from world-class organizations. If it had, the establishment of goals at step six would have been unnecessary. Benchmarking for best practices implies the goal of meeting or surpassing the performance of the best-in-class organization. At PMG's step seven, the importing of practices from partners is implicit in "develop action plan."

These guides give a sense of the variations in benchmarking that currently exist. The deeper you delve for benchmarking procedures, the more variety you will find in the recommended steps, and the less constrained you will be by the directives of any one benchmarking authority.

Our Definitive Process

Having reviewed various guidelines, we have the luxury of choosing which steps to include in our own set. The following list provides a brief explanation for the selection of each step and its position in the list:

1.   *Determine purpose and scope of project.* We chose this step because it is straightforward, so we are taking it verbatim from Pacific Bell (Cartwright, 1995, n.p.). Before choosing benchmarks or partners, an organization has to set limits or boundaries—on time, expenditures, number of benchmarks, number of partners, number of internal processes to be reconfigured, number of people on the benchmarking team and the oversight committee, and so on. This step includes *process triage:* deciding which processes need to be benchmarked and in what priority.

2.   *Know thyself.* Analyze your internal processes to get a thorough understanding of what is really going on. Dig under the surface of the process to grasp the true driving forces behind each performance measure.

3.   *Research potential partners.* It is unlikely that you will have the time or resources to locate every piece of information on possible partners, but typically this method succeeds in gathering enough information for the purposes of benchmarking.

4.   *Choose performance measurements.* Take care to choose a set of measures that are comprehensive yet common for the chosen process or function. The closer you can approximate apples-to-apples, the more secure and valid your findings will be.

5.   *Collect internal data for performance measurements.* Measure current performance.

6.   *Collect data from partner organizations.* Do so with courtesy and as little time and bother as possible, but do not sacrifice data reliability.

7.   *Conduct gap analysis.* Prepare both the benchmarking team and project managers for the possibility of unpleasant results and reactions. Present results to management. Also, follow benchmarking etiquette and share your findings with your partners.

8.   *Import practices in order to close gaps.* Use the borrow-adapt-adopt procedure. Choose the processes, allow for necessary mutations to fit your structure, and implement.

9.   *Monitor results.* Improvements in performance measures should indicate a closing of the gap between the partner's performance and your agency's, and the relative pace of the closing.

10.   *Recalibrate on the basis of findings.*

11.   *Return to step one.* In your initial process you conducted process triage. Now move to the second level of functions that need improvement, and conduct the entire exercise again.

As effective as benchmarking is when performed correctly, misuse of the method is possible. Companies have undertaken benchmarking programs that bear little to no resemblance to a search for best practices. These firms crunch numbers to compare their performance with compatible firms using a predefined set of measures and end up merely revealing the firm's position in the range of the comparison group. Ironically, good results on such indicators tend to discourage managers from striving for excellence (Doades, 1992, p. 16). "We are already better than most others," they say, "so why do we need to improve?" This is a self-deception trap. After data analysis, an organization that is at or near the top and decides to rest on its laurels is lulling itself into a sense of false security and will soon be overtaken by those that rated lower.

Some Results from Benchmarking

Patricia McInturff, director of the regional division of Seattle–King County Department of Public Health, described its partnership with San Francisco on AIDS case management as "stealing everything we could" (Barrett and Greene, 1993, p. 46). McInturff also noted the advantage of having "the luxury of watching their mistakes." San Francisco's glut of case managers made managing cases confusing and difficult, so Seattle centralized and limited the number of case managers and stopped the spread of small agencies by forming a coalition (Barrett and Greene, 1993, p. 47). The city took San Francisco's model and moved it one step forward, significantly improving its performance.

Localities that insist they have no room to maneuver in their budgets need to face this fact: limited resources are not an excuse for stifled progress. Officials in Oklahoma City realized this when they established a "pothole hot line," which drivers can call to report road defects. Thanks to this small, inexpensive program, the city no longer has to send its employees out looking for potholes, and the savings and progress are both significant (Barrett and Greene, 1993, p. 37).

According to consultant William Gay (1992), the Milwaukee, Wisconsin, fire department had a high rate of fire deaths, so it looked at other departments around the country to find one with a program that targeted that issue. Milwaukee found its solution in a smoke detector installation program in Portland, Oregon.

After implementing a modified form of the program, Milwaukee's fire deaths plunged from three per year in targeted neighborhoods to one in five years. Choosing Portland as a benchmark to which it could aspire, Milwaukee successfully followed recommended benchmarking procedures: (1) the team began with a literature search for best practices; (2) Milwaukee officials contacted their Portland counterparts for information; (3) the officials conducted a thorough analysis of the problem, including geographic location, housing, and victim characteristics (the target areas in both Portland and Milwaukee were low-income neighborhoods where residents had limited exposure to fire safety messages on television and radio); and (4) the city adapted the Portland program to its own department (Gay, 1992, p. 30).

Such success stories reinforce the view of C. Jackson Grayson, APQC chairman, that benchmarking "provides the details behind the best practices and enables managers to learn from competitors and those outside their own industry" ("Use TQM," 1994, p. vii). Corporations realized long ago that they are not lone islands in the midst of unnavigable, shark-infested waters. Process ideas now move smoothly and frequently among them. Public sector organizations can benefit immeasurably by adopting this outlook. Once an agency starts benchmarking with external partners, the relationship between various public, private, and other organizations involved in the project becomes cooperative. They share a vision and realize that all partners must work together to effect change. "Barriers between groups that traditionally compete for revenues and budget appropriations will disappear," says John Scully (1995), manager of the Public Innovator Learning Network. For instance, the matter of crime, once treated solely as the purview of the police department, has become a shared concern among social service providers, police, and courts alike. As more agencies and departments begin to benchmark and cooperate with each other, more of these antiquated barriers will fall by the wayside.

Chapter Three

Assessing Organizational Readiness for Benchmarking

A benchmarking team from a large federal agency made a site visit to a private sector firm engaged in identical work. The team spent three days with its benchmarking partner learning how the company performed a specific process. The team members had initially worried that their host would not be completely open and informative because the two organizations were in fairly direct competition. By the end of the visit, however, the team members were delighted with what they had learned. They had been amazed at the amount of information shared and the forthright answers provided to their probing questions. The visiting team leader asked his host how the company could afford to give so much information freely to the benchmark team. Was it not worried about losing its competitive advantage? The host replied, with some embarrassment, that the company was not concerned about sharing the information because it did not believe the visiting team's agency was capable of doing anything with it. The reason, the host explained, was not that his was a private sector organization and the other in the public sector; rather, he did not think that the agency was ready to act on what it learned from the benchmarking process.

Another large federal agency decided to benchmark a process with a private sector company that was world renowned for a best practice. The agency established a high-level executive team to study the process and transfer it back into the organization. After years of effort, tens of millions of dollars spent, and hundreds of staff years expended, the agency still has not imported the practice successfully.

These two agencies encountered difficulties in their benchmarking projects not because there was something inherently different between them and the private sector companies with which they benchmarked. Rather, they had not reached readiness levels in any of the factors that ensure a successful benchmarking experience. They were not culturally, technologically, or psychologically equipped to implement the process. Additionally, they were lacking a thorough understanding of their own systems, and these systems were so entrenched and fixed that the teams could not be open to innovations and new ideas. Readiness is key to a productive benchmarking venture.

Importing a best practice discovered through benchmarking is similar to transplanting an organ. Just as an organ can be rejected by the host for a variety of causes, a best practice can fail to import for many reasons. And just as much of the probability of a successful organ transplant can be maximized, the executives and benchmarking teams in an organization trying to import best practices can do a lot to ensure success.

In an organ transplant, the medical team addresses four types of concerns to minimize the likelihood that a donor organ will be rejected. First, the transplant donor and recipient are matched on various biological and chemical factors (for example, blood type). Second, the organ recipient is prepared for the organ; drugs are used to lower the body's natural defenses against the introduction of foreign tissues. Third, the donor organ is prepared for the transplant. And finally, after the surgery, the recipient is continuously monitored and supported, medically and emotionally, so that the organ and its new environment can adapt to each other. If any sign of rejection occurs, the medical team intervenes swiftly.

In the same way, an agency should match itself fairly closely with a partner in terms of compatibility criteria (for example, same or similar mission, processes, size, culture) and ensure that it has mechanisms in place that allow a successful importation of best practices. Close monitoring of the implementation process is crucial to preventing rejection and sustaining a strong, healthy agency improvement.

The Five Readiness Levels

The activities needed to assess, create, manage, and monitor organizational readiness for importing best practices fall into five broad categories:

1. Benchmarking readiness, which deals with matching the benchmarking organization and its benchmark partners on various dimensions.
2. Culture readiness, which concerns the readiness of the benchmarking organization and its environment for importing the best practice.
3. Implementation readiness, which covers activities that prepare the specific organizational entity and the benchmark practice itself for implementation in the new setting.
4. Operation readiness, which addresses the last and most enduring issues: those that monitor the status and ensure the successful ongoing operation of the practice once it is in place.
5. Technical readiness, which centers on the technical skills needed to conduct a benchmarking study and to import a best practice. Much as a medical team's skills are critical throughout an organ transplant process, the technical readiness of an organization is key to the benchmarking process, from the planning through the operation phase.

Benchmarking Readiness

Benchmarking readiness is determined by two factors: similarity between the benchmarking organization and its partner organization and similarity between the processes being benchmarked in the two organizations. As the similarities increase, benchmarking readiness also increases (see Figure 3.1). Executives and the benchmarking team can ensure successful importing of the best practice by matching the complexity of the best practice with the maturity of the organization in benchmarking.

Organizations with little or no benchmarking experience should first use the process internally to identify and implement their own best practices. A search within the agency for best practices ensures that the organization and process similarities are

Figure 3.1. Benchmarking Readiness Matrix.

	Moderate Benchmark Readiness	**Low Benchmark Readiness**
Highly Dissimilar	Need moderately skilled staff and some benchmarking experience. *Challenge:* Will the best practice from a very different organization work in the benchmarking organization?	Need benchmarking experience and skilled staff to be successful.
	High Benchmark Readiness	**Moderate Benchmark Readiness**
Highly Similar	The best position for acquiring benchmarking experience and developing staff skills.	Need moderately skilled staff and some experience. *Challenge:* Will the best practice from a very different process generalize to the process being benchmarked?

Similarity Between Organization and Partner Organization

Highly Similar　　　　*Highly Dissimilar*

Similarity Between Processes

maximized, thus making the benchmarking itself easier. As an illustration, at the end of each tax filing season, the IRS's Service Center in Ogden, Utah, selects a few specific processes that it wants to improve for the next tax year. The center benchmarks to identify which of the IRS's nine other centers has the best practice, and it then imports that practice. The cost of the benchmarking and importing is minimal, the center continually improves, and the staff develops the skills to benchmark with more diverse organizations and practices.

As an agency gains experience and expertise with benchmarking, the search for best practices typically grows. An organization that has successfully benchmarked internally starts to look outside its own boundaries, first to organizations performing a similar set of activities better, then to those performing a similar set of activities that are the "best" in industry, then to those performing those activities in a world-class fashion.

Similarly, as an agency gains confidence in its benchmarking ability, it seeks out best practices from organizations performing different types of work and tries to improve its processes by understanding and applying what it learns from these different processes. In one of the most documented success stories, Xerox benchmarked selected logistics practices at L. L. Bean, a mail-order retailer. In a lesser-known example, an OB-GYN clinic benchmarked its scheduling practices with a Toyota car assembly plant. The clinic found it had problems scheduling its patients for all the needed tests and maintaining an appropriate inventory of supplies. In thinking about its process, the clinic realized that it was running a nine-month assembly line, much as an automobile assembly plant does. The clinic learned how Toyota scheduled the increasing number of inspections needed as the car neared completion; the clinic's situation was similar in that it had to schedule tests more frequently as women approached their due dates. The clinic also looked at how Toyota planned and stocked its inventory of supplies. Although the applications were different, Toyota's manufacturing practices could be applied to the clinic's scheduling process because the basic principles were extremely similar.

With added experience and confidence, an agency can search for best practices in any field or for any practice worldwide. The ability to learn and improve is limited only by skills, creativity, and commitment. Without sufficient benchmarking readiness, however, organizations will find it difficult and expensive to import best practices. In the second example presented at the beginning of this chapter, a large federal agency was unsuccessful in spite of its best efforts to import a world-class practice. The agency had never benchmarked any other process, had no skills to do the benchmarking, and had an existing process that was radically different from the best practice. If the agency had assessed its benchmarking readiness prior to starting the effort, it would have found a more appropriate partner and process and would have been much more likely to succeed.

We know of another large federal agency that faced similar problems when it considered making a first benchmarking effort with a world-class organization. The agency decided to benchmark its software development process with an organization recognized as the best in class. After talking with the partner organization and making an introductory site visit, the executive in charge of the effort decided to cancel the benchmarking study. He and his team could not relate to the concepts and practices used in the partner organization. The best-practices organization was so far beyond the benchmarking agency that the exercise would have been futile. The executive developed a new strategy aimed at benchmarking organizations more similar to his own in performance level, practice, and mission. As his agency matured, improved its processes, and developed stronger benchmarking skills, the benchmarking studies would expand to include world-class organizations.

Culture Readiness

Once benchmarking readiness has been addressed, an organization must focus on cultural issues that will facilitate or impede the benchmarking process and the successful importing of best practices. These issues stem from the unique values, principles, and norms of each agency. Because each agency has a slightly different culture, each has its own unique set of concerns. Nevertheless, there are a few common cultural norms, each with an impact on benchmarking.

Commitment to Improvement

Organizations need to commit to continuing improvement. Too often they will commit to a particular approach (for example, total quality management, benchmarking, process analysis), and if that approach does not meet expectations, their resolve to improve falters. There is no single approach that will solve all organizational problems. None will invariably improve performance. On the other hand, an agency committed to improvement will continue to try different tools, techniques, and approaches until it achieves the desired improvement. Benchmarking is not the solution to all performance problems; it is, however, a powerful tool in the performance improvement inventory.

Being a Learning Organization

Many organizations suffer from the not-invented-here syndrome. They spend time and energy explaining why a best practice cannot or will not work in their situation rather than finding the ways to make it work. Peter Senge (1990) suggests in *The Fifth Discipline* that the most successful organizations are those that are constantly learning. They systematically find best practices and adapt them to their needs instead of always going through a costly trial-and-error process or conducting their own research and development. Because the essence of benchmarking is an outward as well as an inward search for ideas for improvement, it can bring especially positive cultural change to an organization afflicted with the not-invented-here syndrome.

The danger of trying to import a best practice into an agency with a not-invented-here attitude is that the practice will not be allowed to succeed. Benchmarking sponsors, executives, and teams need to ensure that the best practice has a supportive environment for its implementation. An organization can provide the proper setting by taking the following steps: (1) establish an executive-level sponsor for the best practice; (2) create the expectation in the benchmarking team's charter that the best practice will be implemented (see Exhibit 3.1); (3) make the responsibility and accountability for the successful implementation very clear to everyone in the organization; and (4) constantly reinforce the value of learning from others.

Exhibit 3.1. Charter for Arlington, Texas, Parks and Recreation Department Benchmarking Project, 1994.

- Staff develops a knowledge of benchmarking, its importance, and what it measures.
- Staff will look outside the department to analyze current operations and compare results with organizations that are recognized as being best in class.
- Process improvements will be identified.
- Benchmarking will serve as a means of perpetuating the "continuous improvement" culture within the department.
- Customer satisfaction will improve as a result of studying issues that are most significant to customers.

Source: Heller, 1994, p. 3.

A Sense of Sharing

A sense of sharing in an organization is reflected in a commonly held set of guiding values and principles, open communication, commitment to a common vision and set of priorities, and effective teamwork. Sharing within the organization is as important to successful benchmarking as is sharing with benchmarking partners. The culture of the organization is defined by the shared norms that have become a part of the daily life of everyone from senior managers to frontline staff. To be in a high state of culture readiness, an organization must have a well-established sense of sharing.

Based on our experiences with successful benchmarking efforts, we believe the desirable cultural norms include the following:

- An obsession with delighting the customer
- Open communications between upper management and employees and across the organization
- Empowered employees who can resolve customer issues on the spot
- Commitment to continual improvement
- Decision-making processes that are based on data rather than intuition (or "gut feelings")
- A focus on process improvement and on having the measurements in place to assess process performance

- Visible, involved, and accessible senior leadership
- Teamwork between labor and management and among functional units
- A willingness to invest in human resources through training, recruitment, and professional development
- Established feedback systems that provide continual information about customer needs and satisfaction
- Well-developed and credible planning processes that align the strategic plan with other planning and operational activities
- The ability to see problems as opportunities for improvement

Many of these cultural norms are similar to those espoused in quality management, and many are just plain good management practices. They take on greater importance in benchmarking, however. If benchmarking is to be successful and if a best practice is to be successfully imported, people in the organization need to work in an atmosphere of free and open communication, where everyone is trying to achieve a common goal: delighting the customer.

Internal cultural differences can be just as pervasive as differences between public and private sectors. In West Virginia's One-Stop Business Registration project, the state changed its processes to enable businesses to register once and meet the needs of all state agencies (tax, economic development, environmental protection, and so on) rather than have to register separately with each. One of the biggest challenges was to find a universal form that would meet everyone's needs. In the tax department, for instance, everything revolves around paperwork. In the Department of Environmental Protection, much of the application process is contingent on on-site inspections. These differences made the challenge of finding common ground that much more acute. In addition, most agencies define themselves as autonomous entities and are resistant to relinquishing what they have always viewed as their exclusive domain. Many turf battles arise over confidentiality of files. One agency often has to exercise freedom of information rights vis-à-vis another agency in order to get the information it needs. To deal with some of this departmental infighting and resistance, the West Virginia team that is benchmarking business registration intends to propose statutory mechanisms that would make certain changes a matter of law.

In the first example at the beginning of this chapter, the host organization expressed doubts about the ability of the visiting agency to implement the best practice it was studying. In fact, the agency was not able to implement the practice. Its culture was such that it could not accept the fact that some other company might be doing the process better. The not-invented-here syndrome prevented the agency from even trying to implement the new process. We suspect that if the benchmarking agency had better established its culture readiness, it would have been much more likely to import the best practice successfully.

Implementation Readiness

We discussed benchmarking and culture readiness first because these typically take longer to address and to reach a level sufficient for successful benchmarking. Most organizations, however, tend to jump directly into benchmarking and skip to implementation readiness, spending the majority of their time and effort on the activities needed to adapt the best practice to their organization and to prepare the organization to receive it. Better preparation on benchmarking and culture readiness would decrease the amount of time needed on implementation readiness and increase the likelihood of successfully importing a best practice.

Several key activities must be accomplished during implementation readiness. First, the benchmarking organization and its key stakeholders need to come to a common understanding of the reasons for the study. Second, the agency needs to make sure that its process is analyzed, mapped, and well understood. The process owners and its stakeholders must see the need for change and want to participate in determining the kind of change to be made. Third, an ongoing communication strategy for the organization needs to be developed and implemented. The continuing support of the organization, its executives, employees, union, politicians, special interest groups, and customers is vital for the successful implementation of a best practice.

It is critical for implementation readiness that the benchmarking agency and its key stakeholders (interested politicians, special interest groups, customers) articulate and share a clear and specific set of reasons, expectations, and objectives for the benchmarking study. The overall goal is usually articulated as "to improve," "to find the best practice," or some other motherhood-and-apple-pie phrase. Instead, dialogue around the question, Why are we benchmarking? focuses the effort on the issues that are most important to the organization.

Some agencies are forced to benchmark because of changes wrought by technology. The development of fire-retardant materials and the spread of fire safety procedures are slowly but surely putting many firefighters out of a job. Fire departments are under increasing pressure from the public and local politicians to justify their budgets and the contributions they make to their communities. The Arlington County, Virginia, fire department found itself in this situation and began a search for other services it could provide to its constituents. The department conducted a benchmarking study of other fire departments to seek out their best practices for community services. As a result of the study, the department is now developing neighborhood service plans, not firefighting plans, to serve the community more efficiently.

The reasons for an agency's decision to benchmark derive from its mission. Given that it has a clear and agreed-on statement of mission, performance measures (measures to indicate how well the program is working) flow from the mission statement and objectives. Processes are defined and continually improved to achieve the performance measures, and benchmarking studies are conducted to identify best practices and improve the processes even more.

One of the basic tenets of benchmarking is that the organization must understand its own processes before investigating best practices in other organizations. Not only is it a matter of good benchmarking etiquette, it is the best way to maximize the benefits of benchmarking.

An organization that begins with an understanding of its own processes before looking at other processes reaps a number of benefits. The primary one is that the organization analyzes its situation before making changes. We wager that every organization has an expensive, high-tech machine that someone thought was the solution to a problem and is now quietly gathering dust in a corner. Conducting a structured, disciplined analysis of internal processes before comparing them with other practices and before making any changes dramatically increases the chances of finding a solution that works.

An organization that seeks a thorough grasp of its own processes first will find that the time it spends benchmarking other organizations will be more productive. The team knows what to look for, can quickly identify where there are differences between its processes and those of the other organizations, and can spend time focusing on the critical points in the process being benchmarked. A thorough understanding of one's own processes also demonstrates commitment and seriousness of purpose to benchmarking partners, encouraging them to be more forthcoming with information and ideas.

Are the right people involved in the benchmarking process? As with any other organizational change, if the people affected by the changes are involved in deciding which changes to make, in planning for them, and in implementing them, the changes are more likely to be successful, and those affected by them will be much more committed to making them successful. Process owners must see the need for the changes and want to make them.

For a best practice effort to be successful, an agency must be willing to take greater risks than it probably is used to. The benchmarking study will focus a spotlight on the agency's weaknesses, pointing out where it can do better. Public agencies have an accountability to the public and elected officials that the private sector does not have. This accountability often requires the airing of organizational dirty linen in public settings (for example, at city council meetings, state legislative hearings, and so on). To ensure a successful benchmarking effort, agencies must educate politicians, elected officials, constituent groups, and its own workforce about the purpose and desired outcomes of the benchmarking. The agency needs to be open about the problems it is trying to address and be willing to share the results of the benchmarking with all interested parties. A well-executed outreach and educational program will secure the commitment and support of the stakeholders in the process.

A second type of risk is internal to the benchmarking organization. The organization's managers and employees are being asked to try something different because it worked somewhere else. Some people in the organization will feel as if they are being asked to do this "new thing" almost as an act of faith. "After all," they may say, "it hasn't been done here before!" An intensive educational and communication program will help to allay these concerns. The important message to send repeatedly to this population is that the benchmarking effort is designed to find best practices and ultimately to improve processes; it is a technique for process improvement, not a report card. In West Virginia's Employee Training project, the level of employee acceptance has been dependent on the level of agency buy-in and on how adequately department bosses have supported the project. There has been a steady need to emphasize improving quality, with the focus on process, not people. People like to be challenged and will work hard to be the best. Benchmarking identifies what is the best.

By involving the right people in discussions about the need for change, the goals and objectives of benchmarking, and the risks and benefits of the process, an agency builds a strong support base for the change. The kinds and amount of risk can be negotiated in reasonable, informed, open discussion with as many stakeholders as possible. Thus all parties, not just the benchmarking team or agency, share in the understanding of and commitment to the risk.

The final aspect of implementation readiness, but one of the most important, is a communications plan to keep stakeholders informed about what is happening. Up to this point in benchmarking, the agency has invested considerable time and energy gaining commitment and support from stakeholders. Sometimes the benchmarking team now goes off to conduct its work, and the stakeholders do not hear from it again until the final report is issued. It is essential to communicate frequently, openly, and repeatedly with stakeholders. Briefings, site visits, articles, and formal and informal briefings are all invaluable in keeping constituencies involved in and committed to the benchmarking.

In West Virginia, communications were handled in a unique way. Each of three projects was assigned two teams: a project or work team and an oversight team, made up of upper-management personnel who had been through benchmarking training but were unable to make the same time commitment to the projects as the work teams. Whereas the work teams did the actual benchmarking research, the oversight teams served as guidance counselors, narrowing the scope of each project. Communication between the two teams was an expediency that ensured that the work team stayed focused and on schedule.

Operation Readiness

When the best practice is imported, operation readiness issues become paramount. Operation readiness involves monitoring the ongoing status of the best practice and making sure that it becomes the new way of doing business. Three concerns arise at this stage: having measures in place to monitor the new process, training the process owners and operators, and ensuring continual improvement of the process.

Monitoring Measures

As with any other process, the organization needs performance measures to determine how well the new process is working. Measures are particularly critical for new processes because until they are in operation, no one can be sure exactly how they will work. In an organ transplant, the medical team needs to pay attention to early warning signs of organ rejection, tissue deterioration, or poor functioning of the organ in its host. Paying attention to warning signals is equally vital for imported best practices.

The imported practice may not work as expected in its new organization, or it may need further adaptation to optimize its effectiveness. The process owners and operators for the practice may be more comfortable with (and certainly more knowledgeable about) the old ways of working and may gradually slide back into their old habits. If the new practice does not work as expected almost immediately or if performance pressure mounts on the new process owners, an almost overwhelming cry for a return to the old ways will be heard. The benchmarking team needs to have measures in place that will determine how well the process is working. Then the team can adjust the process to address operational concerns and head off objections before they arise.

Training for Process Owners and Operators

Training for those responsible for the process begins during implementation. The process owners and operators need to know how the new practice works so they can help adjust the process to its new environment and then execute the process as intended. New skills are often forgotten, however, and people can revert to old habits. Thus training and reinforcement on the new process needs to be given periodically during the operation phase. These training sessions also provide great opportunities to get feedback from the process owners and operators on ways to improve the process.

Continual Improvement of the Best Practice

The benchmarking process seeks out and identifies best practices, not perfect practices. After all of the work in finding and importing a new practice, agencies and their staff may be hesitant to change any part of it, treating it as if it is sacred. It is vital for the health and continued improvement of the organization that this new best practice be considered a process to be improved, just like any other process. Benchmarking is a continual search for better ideas, better ways of doing business, improvements in everything we do.

Technical Readiness

Technical readiness refers to the knowledge, skills, ability, and experience available to the agency doing the benchmarking. The expertise may be developed in-house or may be acquired through consultants, contractors, universities, or other external sources. The individuals with these skills help the organization get ready for benchmarking by addressing the issues presented in benchmarking readiness, culture readiness, implementation readiness, and operation readiness, and conduct the benchmarking effort.

The most important issue to be addressed in technical readiness is the availability of the right skills and experience to conduct benchmarking studies. As the rest of the book will discuss, an organization needs to have a knowledge of process analysis, questionnaire and survey design, statistics, how the current process operates, how benchmarking works, and to some extent, how organizations work (organizational behavior). Much of this knowledge will be available in the agency; if it is not, it should probably be acquired externally rather than through new hiring, or it should be developed within the organization.

Benchmarking is a powerful tool in the quest for improvement, but many people either know nothing about it or misunderstand it. It is extremely important for an agency preparing to benchmark to invest the time and resources necessary to educate itself about the benchmarking process. Executives, senior managers, union leaders, process owners, elected officials with an interest in agency affairs, and other stakeholders all need to understand what benchmarking is and is not before a study is undertaken. This learning experience helps to establish realistic expectations, allay fears and doubts, lay the groundwork for broad support, and position the agency for successful benchmarking. An early investment in benchmarking education pays dividends later in the process.

Finally, technical readiness can be improved by having expert help available in case it is needed. Expertise in statistics, survey design, and benchmarking is extremely valuable when problems arise. Professionals with experience in benchmarking can help maximize the benefits of the effort and point out problems to avoid. They will also help to develop internal expertise so the organization can become self-sufficient in benchmarking. Third-party experts are especially helpful in finding benchmarking partners and conducting the data collection with them.

Preparing for Change

A successful benchmarking effort depends on the readiness of the organization to deal with the results, findings, and recommendations that stem from the study. Benchmarking is a quest for better ways to do work and thus is going to cause changes in the agency. To reap the benefits of benchmarking, the agency and its stakeholders must be ready to accept change and make a commitment to implement the new practice. The agency's environment must be open to doing something "not invented here." To prepare the organization for these changes, the agency must make a concerted effort to raise its readiness levels—benchmarking, culture, implementation, operation, and technical. Although we discussed these readiness issues sequentially, they need to be addressed simultaneously. Benchmarking, culture, and technical readiness take longer to prepare, so they need to be started before implementation or operation readiness. As a benchmarking study unfolds, different types of readiness become more and less important, so all five readiness levels need to be cultivated, monitored, and managed throughout the benchmarking process.

By properly preparing the organization for benchmarking, an agency can prevent many problems later in the benchmarking process and can ensure the success of its best practice implementation.

Are You Ready for Benchmarking?

In our work with agencies conducting benchmarking studies, we are frequently asked how an organization can assess its readiness in the five areas we consider essential for a successful effort. To help agencies determine their readiness and guide their attempts to increase their readiness levels, we prepared a series of questions about each readiness area. The psychometric properties of the self-assessment instrument have not yet been analyzed, but the organizations that have used the questions have found them a valuable way of thinking about their readiness for benchmarking.

Some agencies have used the questions to think about and discuss their readiness without scoring themselves at all. Others have used the scoring system as a rough measure of their readiness and an indicator of their relative strengths and weaknesses. We encourage you to use the questions in the way that best suits your needs. Use the results of the self-assessment not to decide whether to benchmark but rather to determine where the agency has readiness risks that can be addressed before or during the benchmarking process. The intent of the self-assessment is to encourage organizations to do the right preliminary work so that they are prepared for benchmarking before the project itself begins.

The following series of questions will give you important information about your agency. Respond to each question with the answer that most accurately portrays the current state of your organization. Then use the results to assess your readiness state and identify the areas where you need to improve your capability to benchmark successfully.

Benchmarking Readiness

Use the following response scale to answer each item. Respond according to the current state of your organizaton.

1 = never; 2 = seldom; 3 = occasionally; 4 = frequently; 5 = always

1. We benchmark internally to find
   our own best practices.   1   2   3   4   5

2. We benchmark with others in our
   line of business to find industry
   best practices.   1   2   3   4   5

3. We benchmark an identical process
   with other agencies to find best
   practices.   1   2   3   4   5

4. We benchmark different processes
   within our own agency to find better
   ways of doing business.   1   2   3   4   5

5. We benchmark an identical process
   with organizations in different lines
   of work to identify best practices.   1   2   3   4   5

6. We benchmark different processes
   with other agencies to find better
   ways of doing business.   1   2   3   4   5

7. We benchmark different processes
   with agencies in different lines of
   work to find better ways of doing
   business.   1   2   3   4   5

8. We benchmark with world-class
   partners to find best practices.   1   2   3   4   5

9. Benchmarking is a process used
   in our agency to find best practices.   1   2   3   4   5

10. We are a world-class or best-in-
    industry agency that others come
    to for benchmarking best practices.   1   2   3   4   5

Scoring: Total the numbers corresponding to your responses; the range of scores goes from 10 to 50. Assess your readiness by determining which of the ranges below your score falls into.

41–50: You are ready to do world-class benchmarking with anyone.

31–40: You are ready to benchmark different processes with organizations doing different kinds of work than your agency does.

21–30: Benchmark with best-in-industry partners, on different processes with agencies in similar lines of work, or on the same process with agencies in different lines of work.

10–20: Benchmark on similar processes and with similar organizations, or do internal benchmarking to develop more skills and experience.

Culture Readiness

Respond to the following items using the response scale below. Answer based on the current state of your organizaton.

1 = strongly disagree; 2 = disagree; 3 = neither agree nor disagree; 4 = agree; 5 = strongly agree

1. My organization is committed to continuous improvement.	1	2	3	4	5
2. People in my work group accept new ideas.	1	2	3	4	5
3. My superiors are receptive to new ideas.	1	2	3	4	5
4. Employees at all levels of this organization believe in continual improvement.	1	2	3	4	5
5. A positive atmosphere of mutual trust and respect between managers and employees exists.	1	2	3	4	5
6. Communications are open in my organization.	1	2	3	4	5
7. The organization supports employee involvement, contributions, and teamwork.	1	2	3	4	5
8. Employees have a strong feeling of empowerment and team ownership of work processes.	1	2	3	4	5
9. A spirit of cooperation and teamwork exists.	1	2	3	4	5
10. We have good relations with other groups and organizations important to our work.	1	2	3	4	5
11. People in my area cooperate with each other to get the job done.	1	2	3	4	5
12. A promising new idea is likely to be approved quickly for a trial.	1	2	3	4	5

13. Taking risks is encouraged.	1	2	3	4	5
14. Creative thinking is rewarded.	1	2	3	4	5
15. Employees are encouraged to find new and better ways to do their work.	1	2	3	4	5
16. It is not really possible to change things.	1	2	3	4	5
17. The organization strives to achieve a common set of goals.	1	2	3	4	5
18. We have a clear understanding of our customers' expectations.	1	2	3	4	5
19. You must avoid making mistakes at all costs.	1	2	3	4	5
20. My unit monitors customer satisfaction on a continual basis.	1	2	3	4	5
21. The organization is dedicated to meeting or exceeding customer expectations.	1	2	3	4	5
22. We have measures to assess how well our processes are working.	1	2	3	4	5
23. My management sees problems as opportunities to improve.	1	2	3	4	5
24. The senior leadership of this organization is very active in communicating the direction the agency is to take.	1	2	3	4	5
25. The organization provides the training and skill development I need to do my job.	1	2	3	4	5

Scoring: For items 16 and 19, reverse the rating score (that is, a *5* response is worth 1 point, a *4* is 2 points, a *3* is 3 points, a *2* is 4 points, and a *1* is 5 points). For all other questions, the response circled and the point value are the same. Total the point values for all of these responses. The total score can range from 25 to 125.

111–125: Your culture readiness is extremely high, and you are ready to benchmark successfully.

91–110: Your readiness level is very good, and you too are ready to benchmark. You probably need to attend to culture issues carefully as the benchmark effort progresses.

70–90: You probably need to address some culture readiness issues before you start benchmarking. Study your responses to the

questionnaire, and note where you rated your organization low. Focus
your attention on those areas for a concerted improvement effort.
Benchmarking at this stage of culture readiness would risk rejection of
the best practice before or during implementation. If your score is
below 75, there are major culture issues that need to be improved
before a benchmark study should be undertaken. Again, study the
items where you rated the organization low, and focus on improving
these areas. A more thorough organizational culture assessment may be
needed to get a better sense of what the issues are and how to improve
your culture readiness.

Implementation Readiness

Respond to the following items using the response scale below. Answer
based on the current state of your organization.

1 = not at all; 2 = to a minimal extent; 3 = to some extent;
4 = to a great extent; 5 = completely

1. My organization understands why
   we are benchmarking.   1   2   3   4   5
2. The current process owners agree
   with the reasons for the
   benchmarking study.   1   2   3   4   5
3. Affected employees are aware of the
   effort.   1   2   3   4   5
4. Interested stakeholders agree on the
   need for benchmarking this process.   1   2   3   4   5
5. Union officials support the bench-
   marking study.   1   2   3   4   5
6. The current process owners are
   committed to the objectives of the
   benchmarking effort.   1   2   3   4   5
7. The benchmarking goals were de-
   rived from the organization's mission.   1   2   3   4   5
8. Owners of the current process
   undertand their process.   1   2   3   4   5
9. The current process is documented
   (mapped).   1   2   3   4   5
10. We have performance measures for
    the current process.   1   2   3   4   5
11. Stakeholders understand the
    benchmarking process.   1   2   3   4   5

12. The organization is willing to share its findings, good and bad, with all stakeholders.	1	2	3	4	5
13. The organization will take significant risks in an effort to improve.	1	2	3	4	5
14. Affected employees know what to expect from benchmarking for best practices.	1	2	3	4	5
15. We know how we will communicate to our stakeholders during the benchmarking study.	1	2	3	4	5
16. The right people are involved in the benchmarking effort.	1	2	3	4	5
17. The elected officials interested in this process understand what benchmarking is to accomplish.	1	2	3	4	5
18. There are no disagreements among stakeholders on the objectives of the benchmarking study.	1	2	3	4	5
19. We know the details of the current process.	1	2	3	4	5
20. Our organization is excellent at keeping employees and stakeholders informed.	1	2	3	4	5

Scoring: Total the numbers you circled for your responses. Total scores may range from 20 to 100.

80–100: You are ready to benchmark and implement your best practices.

65–79: You need to give some attention to improving your implementation readiness, but you are ready to benchmark. Review the items where you rated your organization low, and improve these areas as you benchmark and implement.

50–64: You need to improve your implementation readiness before you start benchmarking. Identify the items where you rated the agency low, and invest your resources in increasing your readiness in these areas. When you have improved on some of these issues, rate yourself again. As your total score rises, you will be ready to benchmark. You need to continue to attend to implementation readiness issues during the benchmarking and best practice implementation process.

Below 50: You are probably not ready to benchmark and need to spend considerable time and effort building a coalition of committed stakeholders to support the benchmarking.

Operation Readiness

Respond to the following items using the response scale below. Answer based on the current state of your organizaton.

1 = strongly disagree; 2 = disagree; 3 = neither agree nor disagree; 4 = agree; 5 = strongly agree

1. We have measures in place to assess the performance of our current process.	1	2	3	4	5
2. We have identified the measures we will use to monitor the operation of the imported practice.	1	2	3	4	5
3. Process owners have been thoroughly trained on the new practice.	1	2	3	4	5
4. The practice to be implemented has been documented in detail.	1	2	3	4	5
5. The employees responsible for doing the new process have been trained on how to do it properly.	1	2	3	4	5
6. The owners of the imported best practices are commited to continuously improving the process.	1	2	3	4	5
7. The individuals doing the new practice have received training on process improvement.	1	2	3	4	5
8. The organization is willing to make changes to perform its processes better.	1	2	3	4	5
9. Process owners and operators know how to use measurement data to make process improvements.	1	2	3	4	5
10. If new ideas do not work as expected, the organization quickly reverts to the tried-and-true methods that do work.	1	2	3	4	5

Scoring: Reverse the scoring for item 10 (a *5* response is scored a 1, a *1* response is scored a 5, and so forth). Total all of the response scores using this new scoring for number 10. Total scores may range from 10 to 50.

40–50: You are in great shape to make the best practice operation successful.

30–39: You are ready to implement and operate the best practice, but you need to pay a little extra attention to operational issues. Make sure sufficient training has been provided and the right process measures are in place and being used.

20–29: You may have operations problems with the new practices. The process owners and operators will need more help, support, and encouragement to be successful. Developing and using appropriate process measures are especially critical because they provide early warning of possible problems.

Below 20: Probably your organization is not ready to operate the imported best practice successfully. You may implement and operate the new process, but the potential for difficulties and possible rejection of the practice is very high.

Technical Readiness

Respond to the following items using the response scale below. Answer based on the current state of your organizaton.

1 = strongly disagree; 2 = disagree; 3 = neither agree nor disagree; 4 = agree; 5 = strongly agree

1. We have staff who have conducted benchmarking studies.   1   2   3   4   5
2. We have access to statistical expertise.   1   2   3   4   5
3. Expert assistance in process analysis is readily available to us.   1   2   3   4   5
4. Benchmarking expertise is available to us.   1   2   3   4   5
5. People in our organization thoroughly understand the process to be benchmarked.   1   2   3   4   5
6. We can obtain expert help to design surveys.   1   2   3   4   5

7. We have worked with external experts
   and/or consultants in previous efforts.   1   2   3   4   5
8. We have considerable experience in
   benchmarking.   1   2   3   4   5
9. Our executives understand what
   benchmarking is all about.   1   2   3   4   5

Scoring: Total the response you gave to each item. The total score may range from 9 to 45.

36–45: Either you have the technical skills needed to benchmark successfully or they are available to you.

26–35: You have access to most of the skills you will need. Review the items in the technical readiness survey, and try to improve the areas where you rated your agency low.

25 and below: Your organization does not have the skills necessary to benchmark. You need to develop those skills internally, identify and use external resources, or decide not to benchmark yet.

Chapter Four

Selecting Practices
to Benchmark

The IRS, for years a leader in the federal government in quality management and benchmarking, was one of the first large public sector agencies to do structured, systematic benchmarking. After it decided to seek out and import best practices, and after some initial training and benchmarking planning, the IRS looked at several different approaches. Rather than overhaul a core strategic process as its first effort, it eventually settled on implementing four demonstration projects: personnel recruitment and retention, software development, responses to taxpayers' requests for forms and publications at form distribution centers, and assistance at taxpayer walk-in sites.

At the local level, Salt Lake City, as part of its quality management initiative, included systematic, formal benchmarking as part of the city's plan to identify and import best practices. To manage and oversee the effort, city officials appointed a group of key stakeholders, including representatives from the mayor's office, to the newly formed Measurement Committee, with the task of creating and monitoring key performance indicators for city services. The committee began its work by identifying thirty-five key processes that were candidates for benchmarking (some of them are listed in Exhibit 4.1) and then established a list of criteria (see Exhibit 4.2) against which to assess each candidate process. Based on this assessment, the committee narrowed the list to two for actual benchmarking: complaint handling and trash and solid waste removal. It brought its selection to the citywide Quality Steering

Committee (which included the mayor and city council representatives) to get its buy-in, approval, and support.

In a case on a broader level, the National Performance Review (NPR) benchmarked telephone service with several private sector partners to identify practices that would help raise the level of telephone service in the federal government to equal the best in business. The NPR (1995, p. 2) gave several reasons for choosing telephone service as one of the first practices to benchmark:

- The large volume of calls to the federal government
- The many agencies that provide a multitude of services over the telephone
- The cost-effectiveness of delivering services over the telephone rather than in person or through correspondence
- The opportunity for improvement
- Support from senior agency leadership
- The fact that agencies had already started some activities to improve telephone service and were ready to improve their services further

As these cases illustrate, different agencies use different decision-making criteria in deciding what processes to benchmark. There is no single correct way, nor is one set of criteria the best in every situation.

Under the West Virginia Inspire Initiative, senior managers who were asked to identify cross-agency issues or areas of improvement listed sixty potential benchmarking areas. West Virginia's benchmarking consultant, Coopers & Lybrand, then conducted an internal strategy audit to help narrow the focus, subsequently reducing the list to twelve areas. Eventually the governor selected three of these areas that he believed were feasible in terms of cost and the projected time line. In the case of Employee Training and One-Stop Business Registration, training and research had been under way for some time.

Four considerations are important to all agencies that are deciding what processes to benchmark:

1. *Readiness issues.* The agency must consider its readiness level and select a process that is appropriate to its readiness.

Exhibit 4.1. Possible Processes for
Benchmarking in Salt Lake City.

- Asphalt patching process
- Complaint handling (problem solving)
- Business permits and applications (inspections, getting permits)
- Baggage handling at the airport
- Snow removal (including from streets, sidewalks, and runways, and salt use)
- Getting from parking to terminals at the airport
- Purchasing
- Neighborhood trash and solid waste pickup
- Street maintenance (overlay; potholes; identify problems; sweeping)
- Crime prevention
- Traffic light synchronization
- Third-party liability claims
- Communication with prosecutors
- Planning and coordinating between utilities and streets
- Cleaning streets
- Educating the public about what we [all the city's departments] do*

*The Measurement Committee eventually decided that "educating the public about what we do" would be analyzed as part of each process selected for the benchmark study.

2. *Strategic issues.* The agency should use its strategic plan to point the benchmarking team toward certain processes.
3. *Customer, competitive, and environmental issues.* These factors may push an agency to benchmark some practices and not others.
4. *Characteristics of the processes.* These characteristics may make one preferable for benchmarking over another.

Readiness Issues

In the case presented at the beginning of this chapter, the IRS decided not to benchmark its major strategic processes because its

Exhibit 4.2. Salt Lake City's Criteria for Prioritizing Candidate Processes.

The selected process should

- Deliver products or services to external customers
- Relate to the city's strategic plan
- Be resource intensive
- Have a reasonable chance for success
- Be visible and viewed as having opportunities to improve
- Be stable; not be in the process of being changed or rebuilt
- Be repeated frequently
- Be controlled by the city
- Be cross-functional
- Have data indicating it is a problem

readiness level was not high enough to ensure success in importing any of these processes. Instead it decided to benchmark simpler processes because it wanted this first benchmarking effort to be successful, and it wanted to gain some experience and expertise before benchmarking more complicated processes.

An organization that is about to embark on the search for best practices must have a clear understanding of where it stands on all five types of readiness. An agency with low benchmarking readiness needs to select a process that it can benchmark internally (or with another extremely similar organization) with an identical process. For instance, an IRS center that processes tax forms should select a process that similar centers perform. Agencies with higher readiness levels might choose more dissimilar benchmarking partners and processes. Some hospitals have tried to improve their check-in procedures by studying hotels, and airline maintenance crews have studied pit crews from the professional automobile racing circuit to improve their maintenance processes.

An organization with low culture readiness may want to select a process that is owned by a part of the organization where the readiness level is somewhat higher. The FDIC's field service centers, for instance, had a much higher culture readiness level than the headquarters office, so the first benchmarking efforts in the agency focused on the processes in these centers.

All of the other readiness levels of an agency—its implementation, operation, and technical readiness—also need to be considered in selecting a process for benchmarking that will have the highest likelihood of being successfully imported. An agency that carefully assesses all five aspects of readiness when deciding what best practice to seek will eliminate many future problems and dramatically increase the chance of successfully importing the new process.

Strategic Issues

During the course of its normal operations, an agency identifies core products and services, activities critical to its success, and many areas ripe for performance improvement. Many of these processes, products, services, activities, and areas have strategic importance to the organization—that is, they are essential to the effective conduct of the organization's business. For example, highway repair is a strategic issue for state departments of transportation because the repairs are essential to the effective execution of the department's core business.

The NPR study selected telephone service as one of the first practices to benchmark partly because of the importance of this service to the public. Tens of millions of the federal government's customers call its agencies every year. Thus, because telephone service is a critical process for the effective functioning of government, it deserves the time, resources, and effort afforded it in a benchmarking study.

After an agency identifies its strategic core business processes, it must determine how the issues that arise in these processes are to be incorporated into the benchmarking selection process. The manner in which the criteria reflecting strategic importance can be expressed varies widely. NPR expressed it as the large number of users; Salt Lake City said the selected process needed to support the strategic plan for the city; the IRS expressed it as one of its core business processes. Regardless of how an organization's strategic issues are included among the criteria for picking a process to benchmark, however, it is essential that these issues be carefully considered.

Customer, Competitive, and Environmental Issues

External pressures are often the driving forces that create the momentum for benchmarking in public sector organizations and key considerations in deciding what to benchmark. Public dissatisfaction, or even outrage, frequently prompts the search for best practices. For instance, a major East Coast city entered into a study of emergency medical services (EMS) after several citizens died waiting for EMS teams to arrive. Competitive pressure, so evident in the trend to privatize public sector activities, can also motivate agencies to seek out and import best practices.

Environmental issues, particularly those arising from the political environment, can really ignite the fire under a benchmarking project. West Virginia's One-Stop Business Registration process had been on the agenda and under research for nine years, but turf battles and legislative restrictions had impeded progress. Not until it was made a benchmarking project and became a mandate of the governor did it become a priority. Press reports, lobbying by special interest groups, and a multitude of other public relations events must be considered in selecting a practice to benchmark. Environmental events can be used to build the mandate needed to effect changes. A winter of record snowfalls helps to galvanize the political body and the public to seek better methods of snow removal, pothole repair, and heating for public housing.

Customer Issues

The focus of all improvement processes, to meet or exceed customers' expectations, is essential to guiding the benchmarking process. One of the criteria the Bertelsmann Foundation uses for its city management award is the demonstrated commitment of the city to its citizens and customers. The criterion assesses the extent to which the local government sees itself as a service provider that gears its services to the needs of its citizens.

The criteria used to express customer issues take many different forms. In Salt Lake City, for example, the impact of the benchmarking on customers was included in two of the criteria: the process selected had to deliver products or services to external customers, and it had to be visible. The Arlington, Texas, parks and recreation department chose four processes for benchmarking that have direct customer impact: round time at city golf courses, the operation of the front desk at recreation centers, athletic field reservations, and customer service systems.

Competitive Issues

With the increased interest of elected officials and the public in privatizing public services, the questions that arise about competition with the private sector are the same that come up in deciding what to benchmark: Can the private sector provide the same or a better product or service for the same or less cost? Is there a firm already providing the product or service? In fact, if certain functions of an organization are candidates for privatization, they are also potential processes for benchmarking. The reasons for privatizing are also the reasons for importing best practices. The solution is quite different, however. In privatizing, you import the agency (or at least some part of its functions) to the best practice, whereas in benchmarking you import the best practice to the agency.

Environmental Issues

Public sector organizations exist in a highly politicized environment, with the spotlight of citizen and press scrutiny ready to illuminate any problem. It would be foolhardy for any agency to decide on a process to benchmark without considering the local political, public, oversight, and press environment and the probable reaction of these constituencies to the benchmarking study.

Significant local events sometimes have a direct effect on the processes selected for benchmarking. Poor response times may dictate the benchmarking of EMS processes. Budget cuts that cause the city government to end its recycling program may create a public outcry for benchmarking recycling processes. Winter traffic problems in northern cities may place snow removal at the top of the benchmarking list.

As these examples illustrate, any number of serendipitous occurrences influence the benchmarking selection process. These events could be seen as nuisances—irrelevant circumstances that should not be considered in the selection of a practice to benchmark—or unique opportunities to mobilize a meaningful and highly invested segment of the populace and interested stakeholders in a collaborative search for best practices.

Characteristics of the Process

A thorough consideration of the context is critical in selecting a process to benchmark, but a number of characteristics of the process itself are equally important:

1. *The process should be meaningful.* It should have a high impact on the customer, preferably the external customer. The benchmarking study needs to be one that will have a significant impact on the users and customers of the process. The selected process should address the needs of the citizens and taxpayers, responding to their concerns about service quality and cost.

2. *The process should be highly visible.* Many people inside and outside the agency should be exposed to some aspect or result of it.

3. *The process should be resource intensive.* It should currently be consuming a large percentage of resources (or time) or bring in a large amount of revenue.

4. *The process should have a history of problems.* Many people need to agree, and data should support the conclusion, that the process or program needs improving.

5. *The process should have the opportunity to improve.* The process needs to have the flexibility to be changed and not be significantly constrained by regulations, statutes, laws, and so forth.

6. *The process needs an environment conducive to change.* Its organizational readiness needs to be high, program or process stakeholders should be receptive to and interested in changes, and the program or process should not be undergoing major revisions or facing serious external threats (for example, lawsuits or litigation).

7. *The process needs to be understood.* The practices should be well documented and mapped, the process should be easily explained, and measures should be in place.

8.   *The process should support the mission, vision, and strategic direction of the agency.* A process to be benchmarked should address business factors critical to the organization, not ones that are peripheral to its success.

9.   *The process should need ideas from other sources to be improved.* If the process can be improved through standard quality improvement tools and techniques or has many clear opportunities for improvement, benchmarking may not be needed. Benchmarking is most effective with processes that have experienced long-term, chronic performance problems and for which process owners and stakeholders have had difficulty finding good ideas for improvement. A search for best practices in these situations expands the pool of possible solutions and fosters creative problem solving.

As this list clearly shows, the criteria for selecting a practice for benchmarking revolve around a relatively basic issue: Is this process worth benchmarking at this time? Practitioners can determine the answer to that question by asking the following questions:

- What is the relationship of the process to meeting customer expectations?
- What are the costs and benefits of improving the process?
- Is improvement possible?
- Is benchmarking the appropriate approach for improving the process?
- Is there a sufficient gap in performance to warrant an investment in benchmarking?
- Are the people who work in the process ready for benchmarking?

The answers to those questions become clear as each proposed process is assessed against the nine benchmarking criteria.

How to Select a Process to Benchmark

The process an agency goes through to select a practice for benchmarking may be even more important than the issues, concerns, characteristics, and criteria it considers in making the selection. The process needs to include all stakeholders in the decision making and provide ample opportunity for dialogue, debate, and discussion with all of them. The likelihood of success for the bench-marking effort depends to a great extent on the consensus that can be reached on criteria for process selection; the clarity achieved on project goals, objectives, and expected outcomes; and the com-mitment gained and maintained from all stakeholders.

Benchmarking efforts can start in innumerable ways. At one extreme the agency has a method of improvement in search of a process: it decides it wants to benchmark and searches for the most appropriate processes. At the other extreme the agency has a process in search of a method: as part of its continuing improvement process, it identifies a process that needs improvement and determines that a search for best practices is the most appropriate method.

Most agencies fall somewhere between these two extremes. They have identified several processes that need improvement and have a set of tools and techniques available to help the change. The challenge is to match the processes needing improvement with the optimal tool or technique. A myriad of ways exist to accomplish this match, but a few key steps are critical to all approaches.

First, the agency lists the most important processes being con-sidered for improvement and benchmarking and describes each in sufficient detail so that employees participating in the decision making have a common understanding of what the process entails (and does not entail). This list of processes is then communicated to the major stakeholders, the process owners, the oversight bod-ies, and key elected officials, who may pare down the list, combine or decompose processes, or add new processes. Eventually a list of processes emerges from this dialogue that is clearly understood and supported by those most involved and interested in the results of the improvement effort.

Second, the agency develops and validates a set of criteria for deciding which processes to benchmark. By examining the readi-ness, strategic, customer, competitive, environmental, and process characteristics issues, the agency identifies the most relevant and important criteria. After it shares these criteria with interested par-ties and constituencies, the list is refined to include only the most important criteria with the strongest support. Reaching agreement on the criteria is often the most difficult and certainly the most crit-ical step in reaching a decision on what practices to benchmark.

Nevertheless time and energy spent to ensure consensus and understanding will prevent many future problems.

Third, the agency assesses each process against each criterion to prioritize the practices. It then presents the top two or three processes as proposed benchmarking projects to the authorizing, oversight, or sponsoring bodies for approval.

Major Benchmarking Pitfalls

Three major mistakes that benchmarking organizations make are the most frequent causes for project difficulties or even failure:

1. The agency assumes that a search for best practices means to look for the best practices in the world and then import them. This naïveté is a sign of low organization readiness. Research and experience suggest that benchmarking with widely dissimilar organizations or on very different processes may actually harm any quality improvement implementation. Practitioners who honestly, thoroughly, and openly appraise their agency's readiness level and select processes for benchmarking that are appropriate for their level avoid the difficulties of being in over their heads.

2. The scope of the practice selected is wrong. Many improvement efforts fail because the topic selected is too broad (for example, simplify taxes), too narrow (simplify item 14 on the tax form), or unclear (make it easier to comply with the tax code). Benchmarking initiatives run into similar problems if the scope of the effort is unclear, too broad, or too narrow. The iterative selection process will help agencies to avoid making this mistake.

3. The agency tries to tackle too many processes at once, so the benchmarking process is not focused. Remember that benchmarking is not the solution for all organizational performance problems nor can it be applied to all the organizational problems for which it is the best approach. An agency needs to focus its benchmarking activities on the critical, strategic processes that most affect the quality and cost of public services. For example, when West Virginia's Employee Training benchmarking team began to consider what aspect of training to focus on, the oversight team gave the benchmarking team a helpful statement of goals: "To ensure that state employees receive the training they need to

deliver quality services to taxpayers; to instill value in training; and to establish a formal 'corporate university' to ensure high quality and consistency in program development, instruction, and administration." The scope of the project was refined after the consultant recommended that the team narrow its focus to process rather than content. The team's mandate became to devise an effective employee training delivery system.

An agency that thoughtfully selects a process to benchmark can avoid these common mistakes. Once that selection has been made, one of the most difficult parts of benchmarking is completed, and the agency is ready to start on the exciting, energizing, and educational phase of the effort. Over the next few months, it will clearly define the process, measure its performance, select benchmarking partners, and come to understand their processes. As with any journey, the route one selects determines what one experiences and learns, the length and expense of the trip, the obstacles or detours encountered, and ultimately whether the destination is reached. The next chapter offers a map for that journey—how to benchmark, how to involve the right groups and individuals in the effort, how to build a strong and productive relationship with benchmarking partners, and finally, how to select and import a best practice.

Part Two

Conducting Benchmarking to Adapt and Implement Best Practices

Chapter Five

The Benchmarking Process Step by Step

One of us was invited on a benchmarking visit to one of the most experienced and successful benchmarking companies in the world. The benchmarking team, a federal agency, appeared to have made all the necessary site visit preparations, including meeting as a team. The members appeared to have done their preparation flawlessly; their enthusiasm was high, and their expectations were even higher.

After arriving and trading pleasantries, the team settled down to a discussion of the process for which it was seeking a best practice. As the hosts asked more and more penetrating questions, the team had fewer and fewer substantive answers. It soon became clear that the visitors were unprepared for a productive site visit with an experienced benchmarking partner. The trip ended with no best practices, few ideas for improvement, and an embarrassed benchmarking team.

This team suffered from the industrial tourist syndrome. Like tourists everywhere, they had planned a visit, coordinated an itinerary, and visited all the top tourist attractions in the host organization's city—but they left with little more than some warm memories to bring home. Industrial tourism (also referred to as "stop-and-shop" benchmarking) occurs when a team approaches a partner without the benefit of adequate research or an understanding of its own processes, hoping to pick and choose a few improvements.

Benchmarking is not industrial tourism, nor is it alchemy, miraculously turning the lead in your agency into gold. It is not yet a science, but it is more than an art. What separates benchmarking from tourism is the formal, structured process that agencies go through in their search for best practices. The more closely and accurately an agency follows this methodology, the more likely it is to find and import best practices successfully.

As we noted in Chapter Two, different organizations and writers have described the steps in benchmarking in a variety of ways. Some list only four steps, others as many as twelve. The number of steps in the process and the exact description of those steps, however, are not nearly as important as the following critical activities:

1. Deciding what process to benchmark and thoroughly understanding this process
2. Selecting benchmarking partners and understanding their practices completely
3. Comparing the identified process with the processes of benchmarking partners to determine where the processes are different and how to change the identified process to improve it
4. Importing the practice and monitoring its performance

We have expanded these four activities into an eleven-step methodology:

1. Determine the purpose and scope of the project.
2. Understand your own process.
3. Research potential benchmarking partners.
4. Choose performance measures.
5. Collect internal data on performance measurements.
6. Collect data from partner organizations.
7. Conduct gap analysis.
8. Import practices to close performance gaps.
9. Monitor results.
10. Recalibrate based on findings.
11. Start the search anew.

Even a first-time benchmarking agency will be able to import a best practice successfully if it follows these eleven steps carefully.

Benchmarking Methodology

To avoid many of the problems that can be encountered in benchmarking and to identify best practices to import, it is imperative that agencies adopt a methodology and then adhere to it. Just as measurement is the process of assigning numbers to something according to a defined set of rules, benchmarking is the process of searching for best practices according to a set of defined rules. The rules are defined by the methodology used. An agency that develops and uses a formal, structured methodology ensures that it is benchmarking, not being an industrial tourist.

1. Determine the Purpose and Scope of the Project

After an agency selects a process, product, service, or function for benchmarking, it needs to articulate the purpose and scope clearly. The purpose describes why it is benchmarking the practice and what it hopes to accomplish. The scope delineates the breadth, depth, time, resources, and other parameters placed on the benchmarking project.

Deciding what to benchmark does not define the purpose of the project. An agency may benchmark the same process for many different reasons, hoping to achieve many different results. Suppose a state decided to benchmark its driver's license application process. The purpose of the project could be to decrease cycle time, increase customer satisfaction, decrease cost, or reduce the number of accidents or the number of driving-under-the-influence infractions. Some of the reasons for benchmarking may actually conflict with the expected results. For example, reducing cycle time might cause higher costs if more staff or better equipment is needed. It is critical to the success of the benchmarking project that all those involved debate its purpose (the reasons for doing it and the expectations for it) and agree on and document that purpose before the project gets started.

The written scope of a project must delineate clear boundaries for exactly what the project should study. There may also be time, resources, or other limits placed on the project, but certain key questions have to be answered—for example, Where does the process being benchmarked begin? Where does it end? What are the limits of this process that separate it from other processes?

A clearly defined scope that is carefully controlled throughout the project is essential to successful benchmarking. Scopes that are too broad or too narrow or suffer "scope creep" cause many benchmarking efforts to founder. In the driver's license application process, does the process begin when the state mails out the application?

When the citizen receives the notice? When the citizen sends in an application? When the state receives the application? The answer to a relatively simple question—Where does the process begin?—will have a dramatic effect on the results expected, the partners chosen for benchmarking, and the kinds of best practices that are found. Similar issues—concerning, for example, where the process ends, its relationships to other processes, how much time the project has, and whether legislative changes are acceptable—must be addressed if the project is to proceed efficiently.

Scope creep is the scourge of many benchmarking projects. When the project starts, a clear, tightly defined scope usually has been established. But as the work gets under way, members of the project team, stakeholders, benchmarking partners, and numerous other interested parties find other processes they want the benchmarking team to look at. Soon the scope has become unwieldy, the focus of the project has been lost, and the additional burden placed on the project brings it to its knees.

Changes to the project purpose or scope need to be managed just as closely as the benchmarking effort itself. Proposed changes should go through the same type of scrutiny, discussion, and decision making that were used to develop selection criteria for potential benchmarking topics, to identify a process for benchmarking, and to come to agreement on the need to conduct a benchmarking study in the first place.

Once determined, a project's purpose and scope are set out in a project charter, which serves as a contract between the agency and the benchmarking team. It communicates to the team not only the project's purpose and scope but also what the team is expected to do, what deliverables it is to produce, to whom it reports, how often the team is expected to provide interim reports, and any time, resources, and other constraints placed on it. Project charters often identify the resources available to the team, the names of the benchmarking team members, an executive contact person for the team, milestone dates for the deliverables, and a brief summary of why the process was selected for benchmarking. Charters can include any information the agency decides is needed to direct and manage the project. Changes in project purpose, scope, resources, timeliness constraints, or any other aspects of the benchmarking project need to be approved by the agency and documented in the charter. The charter thus provides the background and history of the project (information that can prove invaluable as the project proceeds) and serves as a guideline for assessing the work of the team during and after the benchmarking.

2. Understand Your Own Process

Once the project purpose and scope have been agreed on and documented in the project charter, the benchmarking team begins its work. It first acquires a thorough understanding of its charter by studying the document, talking to the individuals or body that developed the charter, and interviewing process owners and stakeholders. The team studies the mission, goals, and objectives of the functional area(s) within which the process operates, and it relates the process it is studying to corporate or strategic goals. It then identifies the customers for the process's outputs and, with the customers, defines their requirements for the process.

Eventually the team draws a detailed map, or flowchart, that displays each step in the process, the location of decision points, the way work moves through the process, and the relationship between the process and other processes (for example, boundaries, places where the process interacts with other processes, where inputs from other processes enter the process, and where the outputs from the process go). Some project teams attach performance measures to the process or steps in the process. In the driver's license example, the team may know that the overall cycle time for the process is twenty-one days and that the first step (opening the mail) takes one day, the second step (routing the mail to the correct location) takes two days, the third step (processing the application) takes ten days, the fourth step (processing the check) takes five days, and the last step (mailing out the new license) takes three days.

During this learning period, the team begins to develop ideas about process bottlenecks, problems, and opportunities for improvement. The team also starts to collect performance measures for the process and to determine the key criteria for success in the process (reliability, cycle time, quality of output, safety, perceived fairness to the public, and so forth). All of this information should be catalogued for future use.

Finally, as part of discovering and understanding its own process, the team identifies certain information that it needs from benchmarking partners in order to gain insight into their processes. The team should winnow the information needs down to twenty-five to thirty questions that team members can ask potential comparison partners over the telephone. The questions, which should be kept fairly simple, typically request readily available information and focus on attaining a description of the other organization's current process. The answers to these questions will be used later to help the team select the most appropriate benchmarking partners.

At the end of this step, the team will have a detailed map of its own process, some potential performance measures for the process, some information needs and a list of questions to obtain that information, and ideas about areas for improvement. The team uses all of this information and develops a project plan for the rest of the benchmarking steps. The plan specifies what needs to be done, when, and by whom. Many plans also describe the expected (or needed) products from each task the team undertakes. This plan serves as the road map for the rest of the benchmarking project; thus, significant changes to the plan should be made with the same care and consideration as are given to changes in purpose and scope. Scope creep often occurs during the execution of the plan, and the only way to keep the scope manageable is to control the changes to the plan.

3. Research Potential Benchmarking Partners

At this stage of the methodology, the search for potential benchmarking partners begins, typically with a fairly long list of possibilities. To create this list, the benchmarking team conducts an extensive review of the literature, contacts associations, interviews experts in the field, posts announcements on electronic bulletin boards or in printed material (magazines and newsletters, for example), advertises at conferences, hires a consultant to help in the search, and generally gathers data from as many sources as possible. The purpose of data collection is to determine what is going on in the field and what other agencies, organizations, or governments are doing in the specific area the team is benchmarking. The search cannot be exhaustive, but it does need to be thorough because it is critical to identifying the right partners for benchmarking.

From all of the information obtained in this search, the team identifies forty to fifty potential partners. The team then generates a list of criteria to be used to narrow this list down somewhat. Many of the criteria tend to consist of demographic similarities: size of government, number of citizens, type of government (for example, centralized versus decentralized, mayor versus city manager), services provided (for example, snow removal, management of an airport, city-operated cemeteries). The other criteria vary with the type of process being benchmarked. For example, in benchmarking for solid waste removal, whether another agency has a recycling program may be a significant issue. If software development is being benchmarked, whether the other organizations are primarily mainframe or client-server based may be a meaningful criterion.

Choosing the right criteria will ensure that the organizations that are potential partners are similar to yours on key dimensions. In searching for benchmarking partners for its snow removal process, for example, Salt Lake City believed that its hilly terrain was a significant factor. Thus, one of the criteria for narrowing its list of potential partners was their "hilliness."

Each potential partner is rated on each criterion. Some of the ratings may be pass-fail. If an agency does not meet a criterion, it is eliminated as a possible partner. Other ratings may be on a scale. For example, if a city wants to benchmark with another city that offers similar recreational activities, the potential partners may receive five points for offering boating, five for skiing, five for swimming, and so on. The more points, the higher the rating and the greater the similarity. The top fifteen to twenty possible partners are selected on the basis of these ratings.

At this point, the team needs more detailed information about some of the other agencies. Once again it determines the criteria for selecting the most appropriate partner, the information it needs to assess each partner against the criteria, and how best to obtain the necessary data.

One major component of the information needed is the performance of possible partners on the processes being benchmarked. In the next three steps of the methodology, we discuss how to identify performance measures, collect internal data on performance, and collect data from potential partners on the key performance measures.

4. Choose Performance Measures

Performance measures are the vital indicators of how an agency, program, process, or function is operating. They quantify the variables, activities, outputs, results, and other aspects of a process that are essential to its performance. They also quantify the criteria that account for the performance of the process. Performance measures are the numbers used to compare the operation of the process being benchmarked with the performance of the benchmark partners' processes.

The benchmarking team members develop a list of potential performance measures, much as they developed the list of possible benchmark partners. By studying their own performance measures, reviewing the literature, talking to experts and others in professional associations, and reading previous benchmark or performance measurement studies, they can generate a fairly extensive list of measures. Although the examination of measures used in earlier studies is a good way to start generating a list, the team should not rely solely on previously used measures. They also need to create new measures that focus on the key variables driving the process that is being scrutinized.

In West Virginia's Measuring Customer Satisfaction project, the benchmarking team worked with its consultant, Coopers & Lybrand, to come up with a best practices hypothesis to serve as the framework for the baseline survey. But the team had devised this hypothesis before research was actually conducted, and as it continued the partner research, it realized that its initial hypothesis was too theoretical and did not jibe with the information it had collected. It came up with second and third sets of best practice hypotheses as it adapted and refined the performance measures.

Once a thorough list of performance measures has been developed, the list needs to be cut down to a manageable size, because the more measures used, the more resource intensive the benchmarking will be. The measures selected should at least cover the key steps in the process being benchmarked and the variables that most affect the process. As resources and time allow, a few more measures may be added to the list. The benchmarking team must recognize, however, that some potential partners may not want to participate in the study if the data collection requirements are too extensive. Thus the team should seek to balance its need for data with the practical matters of cost, time, and partner willingness.

5. Collect Internal Data on Performance Measurement

Just as the benchmarking team should fully understand its own process before studying another organization's practices, it should know how the performance of its own process measures up before asking other agencies to share their performance measurement data. Therefore, it applies the performance measurements selected in step four to the process, function, or service selected for benchmarking. It should be sure that when it compares its own agency with its benchmarking partners, it is looking at similar things (comparing apples with apples) and measuring them the same way.

6. Collect Data from Partner Organizations

For each potential partner remaining on the list, the team now collects data on performance measures. The first step is to study the publicly available literature and data sources. If the team is unable to find the data it needs in that way, members can call the agency, explain the benchmarking study, and request the information needed. Readily available information is often provided over the telephone. A short, focused questionnaire or survey form that is provided to the organizations will often yield the rest of the information needed.

The benchmarking team now compares the performance measures from its own agency with the performance data from the potential partner agencies. The team does not need data on every performance measure from every partner to conduct this comparison, but the more complete the data are, the better the comparison will be. This comparison helps to narrow the list of potential benchmarking partners by identifying the organizations whose performance measures are significantly better. By now the list of potential partners should be pared down to about five or six organizations that have met the selection criteria and whose performance measures suggest their practices are better than those of the benchmarking agency.

These five or six agencies are the benchmarking partners. The benchmarking team will work with the agencies that agree to become partners, seeking to understand their processes, determine how such processes differ from those of the team's own organization, and identify the elements that make an agency's performance a best practice. Partners will assist in identifying best practices that can be imported into the benchmarking agency to improve its performance. Data collection efforts will be much more extensive, possibly extending to site visits, in which the benchmarking team goes to the partner organization to observe and study its process. Site visits afford both organizations the opportunity to share information and ideas, explore alternative practices, and synergistically generate possibilities for even better practices. This part of benchmarking is the most fun, the most rewarding, and the payoff for all the hard work that has been done to get this far. It is also the essence of the search for best practices and so important that we have devoted most of the rest of the book to it.

7. Conduct Gap Analysis

Gap analysis identifies the differences between your process and that of your benchmarking partners. The gap may be a performance difference, reflected in the performance measures, or it may be a process difference, indicated by differences in how the process operates. For example, when Salt Lake City and Reno together benchmarked the customer service systems of Charlotte and Seattle, the teams found that Charlotte forwarded complaints to the responsible organization for resolution, whereas Seattle had a group of complaint investigators in the Citizen Service Bureau who looked into the complaints and facilitated their resolution. Although the processes that the two cities used were similar, significant differences like this one became apparent during the gap analysis.

The goal of the gap analysis is not for the benchmarking team to identify differences between it and its partners but to understand why there are differences. What about one process makes it better than another? What practices produce better performance? What are the drivers of the performance measures? The search for answers to these questions leads to the identification of best practices. By determining what factors make one process operate better than another, the team also finds the information it needs to change those factors in its own organization.

8. Import Practices to Close Gaps

Once the benchmarking team has identified a practice or practices that can improve its performance, its organization prepares to import the best practice. Sometimes the practice can be introduced exactly as it is carried out in the partner organization, but usually a practice needs some modification to fit the new organization. There is no need to wait until the entire benchmarking study is completed before introducing a new practice. If the team finds a best practice that can be imported immediately and will improve the process right away, it can go ahead and use it.

The gap analysis identifies where the benchmarking team's agency can improve and some of the required changes to bring about this improvement. This information needs to be translated into specific actions, milestones, and responsible individuals if it is to be successfully used to improve performance, however. Thus the benchmarking team needs to develop an action plan for implementing the best practices that clearly states the action to be taken, when it needs to be done, and who is to do it.

One of the great obstacles to organizational change is the inevitable resistance of those being asked to make the change. They cannot be allowed to prevent the introduction of the new process. If a best practice is to be implemented successfully, the managers, employees, stackholders, and other interested parties must be included in the decision and implementation process. Sharing the data from the benchmarking study, the gap analysis, the best practice, and the plans for importing the practice with all of these constituencies will elicit their support and involvement, which are essential to the success of the new best practice. The managers and employees who are using the current process are often especially helpful in figuring out how to import the best practice.

An exceptionally good benchmarking study will nevertheless be a failure if the best practice is not imported successfully. Agencies typically are very good at conducting studies but often weak at the hard work and follow-through needed to make the recommendations from those studies take root in the organization.

9. Monitor Results

A recently imported best practice requires special care, attention, and nurturing; otherwise it runs the risk of fading away or regressing back into the previous process from lack of support and follow-through. The benchmarking sponsor, team, and stakeholders need to be especially vigilant during the implementation and early operation of the new practice to ensure that it is installed in a way that is faithful to its design (that is, that the practice is implemented and operated the way the benchmarking study recommended) and that the practice is producing the intended results.

Many organizations pilot-test new processes and monitor the objectives and results closely to answer a number of important questions:

Are the objectives reasonable given the pilot-test situation?

Are the objectives achievable?

Does the pilot give the best practice an opportunity to achieve its best results?

What are the results of the pilot?

Did it achieve the expected performance level? If not, why not?

Were there any unanticipated consequences?

What effect did the process have on the processes with which it interacted?

When the best practice is implemented fully in the organization, both the way in which it is implemented and the results it is achieving are followed carefully. The best practice needs to be installed in the way that was intended, and the factors affecting the success of the new process need to be watched and adjusted as needed. Are the operators of the new process sufficiently trained? Do the owners of the process receive accurate, timely feedback on the operation of the process? How are the processes that provide input to and take output from the new process handling the new way of doing work? What are the performance measures for the new process? Is it achieving what was intended?

The ultimate measure of the success of a best practice is whether the performance measures for the process improve. After all, the search for best practices is not an academic exercise; it is a means to an end—a way to improve organizational performance. If performance measures do not reflect improvement, you can get to the source of the problem in several ways. You can examine the process to see if it was implemented properly or needs to be modified to provide its full benefit in the new setting; or you may need to study the processes and systems surrounding the new practice to see if they are having an adverse effect on the process. New processes sometimes take a while to reach full performance, so the performance measures can be tracked over time to determine if the process is improving.

In some cases, the measurement system itself has to be reconsidered. The measures used for the old process may not make sense or may not be comparable in the new process. Be wary about changing measures, however; a change in measures is often used to obscure the poor performance of the new practice. Thus a reconsideration of the measurement system should be a last resort. It is better to develop strong performance measures, stick with them through the implementation of a new practice, and figure out why the practice is not delivering what the benchmarking study indicated it should.

In most cases, particularly if the benchmarking study is conducted well, the performance measures will show improvement. The new practice needs to become institutionalized (that is, become the way of doing things), performance measures need to be monitored and tracked to ensure that the higher level of performance is sustained, and continual improvement principles need to be applied to improve the process.

10. Recalibrate Based on Findings

Successfully importing a best practice changes the way the agency does its work and frequently even changes its culture. A new best practice certainly changes the results obtained on performance measures (if it did not, it would not be a successful implementation).

Over time the environment within which the practice operates changes, as does the competitive world outside the agency. Healthy benchmarking programs need to be monitored, assessed, and recalibrated periodically to determine the effects of all these changes on the best practice and to evaluate progress on benchmarking goals and objectives.

Recalibration means essentially doing a mini-benchmarking study. The agency goes through all the steps of the methodology to understand its own new process, conducts a gap analysis, and identifies opportunities for performance improvement. Performance measures are reassessed, and the expected levels of performance on the measures are raised to account for the results achieved with the imported best practice. To the extent that the owners of the process keep up with the process, its performance measures, changes in the external competitive arena, and the rest of the information gathered in the original benchmarking study, the recalibration exercise requires less time and fewer resources. The ultimate goal is to have benchmarking be a continual process in which recalibration is a standard operating practice rather than a special activity done every year or two.

11. Start the Search Anew

Benchmarking is the continual search for best practices to improve organizational performance. As soon as an agency implements a best practice, the opportunity to improve that process exists. As practitioners gain greater experience, expertise, and confidence with benchmarking, they can widen the search for best practices to more diverse organizations and processes. There are no perfect practices; every process can stand improvement. Thus, the search for best practices continues. The power, vitality, creativity, and performance that benchmarking can bring to an organization are limited only by its willingness to conduct the quest.

A Dose of Reality

The methodology we have recommended requires discipline, some sophistication in its use and application, and considerable effort and resources. Not all benchmarking efforts are worth this formal, structured approach, nor is this the only way to find best practices to improve your agency's performance.

Furthermore, the methodology is the means to an end, not the end in itself. Benchmarkers need to keep in mind why they are benchmarking and to identify and import best practices, but they should not be so wedded to the methodology that they become tied up in completing each step just to be faithful to it. The following general guidelines for benchmarking will help put the methodology and its application in perspective.

Develop a methodology that works for your organization. It should be appropriate to your agency's culture and level of experience in benchmarking. The specific methodology used is not nearly as critical as having a methodology and adhering to it. By tailoring an approach to your circumstances—and perhaps even developing the methodology participatively—you will increase your organization's commitment to and understanding of your methodology.

Follow the methodology religiously unless. . . . Following the methodology closely helps to ensure that a valid best practice is found and imported successfully. To the extent that shortcuts are taken and the methodology bypassed, the benchmarking effort opens itself up to spurious findings, to practices that are not best and will not improve organizational performance, and to costly failures.

Benchmarking is essentially applied research; it is using the scientific method to try to find factors (variables) that affect the performance (results) of organizational processes. Thus the more closely the methodology follows the rules and procedures of the scientific method, the better and the more conscientiously the methodology is applied, the more likely you are to find and successfully import best practices.

If you find a practice that clearly is overwhelmingly better than your current process, do not analyze it to death before implementing it (or at least trying it out in a pilot test). The risks of deviating from the methodology need to be balanced against the cost of the benchmarking study and the potential benefits from implementing a best practice. The goal in benchmarking is not to find scientific truths; it is to improve organizational performance.

Keep the purpose of benchmarking in mind constantly. As the benchmarking effort gets into full swing, those employees deeply involved in it sometimes lose sight of why they are benchmarking. Keeping the goal of benchmarking, to improve performance, in focus at all times will help to eliminate several problems that occasionally arise. For instance, during the definition of performance measures and data collection phases of the methodology, benchmarking teams often become derailed trying to obtain unnecessary precision in their measurements. Sometimes the wise choice is to settle for rough measures rather than accuracy to several decimal places.

Another common problem is that teams start to focus on a small piece of the process rather than the process as a whole. As a result, their recommendations tend to optimize that piece of the process but suboptimize the whole process. If you keep the bench-marking effort firmly rooted in its primary purpose—to identify and import best practices—you can avoid these pitfalls.

Be sure that the benchmarking team has the right skills. Much of the value of benchmarking comes from the insights and understanding gained through the effort. Data, numbers, measures, process flow diagrams, and all the other tools and techniques of the trade provide input for creative, intelligent analysis by your benchmarking team. Because benchmarking is a process in which individuals generalize from one set of circumstances to a different set, the benchmarking team members should be selected for their analytic skills, their ability to see similarities in dissimilar situations, and their ability to generalize their observations from one setting to a different one. An organization's success in finding and importing best practices relies as much on the insight and creativity of the benchmarking team as it does on the methodology.

Benchmarking is a process and needs to be continually improved. Indeed the benchmarking process itself can be bench-marked and continually improved. As the agency gains experience with its methodology, it will change some steps or activities, add others, and eliminate yet others. Once it has benchmarked several processes and successfully imported the identified best practices, it may want to benchmark its benchmarking process with partner organizations that have recognized best practices. The benefits accrue faster and in greater number as the agency becomes better at benchmarking; soon benchmarking becomes a way of organizational life.

Chapter Six

Building Benchmarking Teams and Political Support

The question of which people to involve in a benchmarking project is a far more serious one for public agencies than for private sector organizations. A benchmarking project in the private sector that is well supported internally is unlikely to be affected by any outside forces. Not so in the public sector, where both internal and external influences must be considered from the beginning of the project. A greater variety of groups, individuals, and situations have a greater opportunity to derail any public sector benchmarking project.

This public scrutiny gives rise to the following questions: What are the reasons for spending time and energy to get others involved? Who should be involved? What will these people contribute? When in the project's time line should they be included? The more thought that is given to these questions, the greater likelihood there is that support for the project will be widespread. Thinking through these questions will also help to ensure that the project is based on identified customer needs rather than on the personal agendas of politicians and other forces in the community.

Why Involve Others?

Several significant benefits accrue to an organization that involves others in the benchmarking project:

1. It will get a broader perspective on what is important to the overall organization and an indication of the most valuable results.

2. Internal and external support from others will help drive the project through completion.
3. People who are involved tend to have a greater commitment to long-term success.
4. The agency will be able to draw from the technical or substantive knowledge held by a variety of people.
5. Involving others is consistent with good leadership, management, and communication principles.
6. The results will be more reliable and valid.

Despite these benefits of involving a variety of people, no benchmarking project should be a free-for-all when it comes to asking people to participate. Project owners should give careful thought to when, why, and how to involve others. Salt Lake City and Reno used a careful, inclusive approach when they teamed up to benchmark the customer referral process.

Salt Lake City's Citywide Quality Management Steering Committee had been implementing quality management for about eighteen months when it undertook the benchmarking study with Reno, its first formal benchmarking partner. By then the Salt Lake City team was well grounded in basic process analysis tools and customer focus. Moreover, it had established a measurement committee, whose members became the sponsors of the benchmarking initiative. The mayor of Salt Lake City was the chair of the steering committee, and a member of the city council also sat on the committee. The measurement committee included a representative from the council's staff. Salt Lake City involved the right people from the beginning, and it continues to do so today.

The timing for Reno's entry into benchmarking was more compressed. Always on the lookout for cutting-edge techniques, senior managers in the city government attended a benchmarking training given by the Innovation Group, a consulting firm. A month later, Clay Holstein, city manager of Reno, was approached by the iKon Group and asked if Reno would join Salt Lake City to benchmark customer referral processes in other cities. After talking with his leadership team, Holstein took advantage of the momentum and moved ahead as a partner with Salt Lake City. He appointed a small team to spearhead the project, which included a champion,

Bill Thomas, director of community development; a technical adviser, Randy Baxley; and a management analyst, Carol Peterson. The city council was supportive because its attention increasingly had centered on how the city responded to constituent complaints. Thus, for the Salt Lake City and Reno partnership, the timing was right, and most key players were already involved.

An agency must make sure that its initial meeting with local politicians is not an open invitation to them to make suggestions. To do so gives the appearance of being unprepared and uninformed as to their interests. It is likely that politicians, especially those who have come from the private sector, will be familiar with the term *benchmarking* but not the details, so those holding this meeting should plan to review the key steps and benefits of a benchmarking study and explain why benchmarking is an important method to use. Next, those in the agency should present the data or explanations that justify their interest in benchmarking the particular process under consideration. Then they should seek the commitment of the politicians by asking if there is a way to gain their support for the project and whether they would consider placing the study on their agenda. The agency personnel should be prepared to explain whether they anticipate that any improvement ideas will require legislative or regulatory changes.

Who Should Be Involved?

The most basic difference between public and private sector benchmarking lies in the two groups of individuals who will be involved in virtually any public sector benchmarking project: politicians and the public, who are significant stakeholders and can provide valuable insight into priorities for improvements and service or product performance goals. Also involved in the process, of course, will be appointed leaders and career managers in the area to be benchmarked; they will provide the process, history, and policy knowledge. We are not advocating that anyone and everyone should be involved. Rather, the benchmarking team should give considerable thought to involving the right people at the right time to ensure success. But who are the right people, and to what end should they be involved? Exhibit 6.1 summarizes the answer to this important question.

Exhibit 6.1. Whom to Involve.

Activity	Group							
	Elected and Appointed Officials	Senior Career Officials	Customers and Stakeholders	Existing Councils or Groups	Champion	Process Owners	Administration Budget Audit Staff	Team Members
Readiness Assessment	•				•	•	•	
Methodology								
1. Determine purpose and scope	•	•	•	•	•	•		•
2. Understand your own process		•	•	•	•	•		•
3. Research partners	•	•	•	•	•	•		•
4. Choose performance measures			•	•	•	•		•
5. Collect internal data					•	•	•	•
6. Collect data from partner						•		•
7. Conduct gap analysis					•	•		•
8. Import practices	•	•	•	•	•	•		•
9. Monitor results	•	•	•	•	•	•	•	•
10. Recalibrate based on findings						•		•
11. Start the search anew	•	•	•	•		•		•

Elected and Appointed Officials

Elected and appointed officials should be consulted at three points in the benchmarking project. The first time is during readiness assessment, to solicit their ideas and opinions about such matters as the following:

- Use of private sector methodologies such as benchmarking
- Opportunities to improve
- Priorities for customer service and products
- Measuring performance
- Sustaining changes over the long run

In these discussions, the team begins to build the coalitions that will be vital to the long-term implementation of improvements. In West Virginia the benchmarking initiatives started at the highest level, with the governor, and worked their way down through the state agencies. This top-down support sent a clear message that the administration was serious about using benchmarking as a method to bring about improvements. In Salt Lake City a representative from the office of the city council assisted in the readiness assessment, helped define the scope and function of the project, and participated in the site visits.

The second point at which elected or appointed officials should be involved is when the team defines the purpose and scope of the benchmarking project. The team should have specific ideas of which processes to benchmark before discussing the topic with officials. The Salt Lake City team identified its top three choices, then sought the opinion of the mayor and council members. Because previous discussions about the benchmarking project had paved the way, the mayor and council members agreed that the team's top choice, the customer referral process, was the best choice.

Elected and appointed officials may have ideas about potential benchmarking partners, surely a mixed blessing for the team. On the positive side, the political network may yield contacts high in the partner organization, virtually ensuring its cooperation and support. But politicians may also nudge the benchmarking team in a certain direction because of the politicians' own interests and ambitions rather than because of the appropriateness of the potential partner. Nevertheless, no matter what the case, enlisting the support of elected or appointed officials from the beginning positions the team to get their assistance during the project, especially if resources are difficult to come by and potential payoffs look good.

Most public organizations are not lucky enough to have the most senior political leader behind the benchmarking effort. His or her attention is typically focused on setting the vision for improvement rather than on the tools used to achieve it. The exception may be municipalities run by a city manager. City managers, in fact, may be expected both to set the vision and to use the latest methods, such as benchmarking, to find ways to improve. Placing a small item on the council agenda may be all he or she needs to do to get the benchmarking ball rolling. Before Reno's benchmarking effort started, its city manager, Clay Holstein, had already publicly identified the customer referral process for benchmarking when he asked for funding support from the seven-member city council. According to Holstein, an explanation of the purpose and expected outcomes of benchmarking were enough to get the council's support, especially because an improvement in customer service is difficult to argue against.

Conversely, several years ago, O. Wendall White, Charlotte's city manager, wanted to benchmark the customer service function to create a blueprint for a new city customer service center. A city manager who strongly emphasizes competitive government, he wanted to learn from Duke Power Company and other nearby private sector firms. Unfortunately local politicians were not enthusiastic about the idea of a customer service center, so he went underground. He assigned a high-energy staff person to visit private sector firms, look for best practices to apply to a customer service center, and develop a center behind the scenes. She did so, and two years later the center was unveiled as part of regular operations. Since then, political support has been more forthcoming.

Senior Leaders

Department or division heads are likely to be the ones who initiate the benchmarking study. Although this level is a good place to start, it is important that such senior leaders assess the readiness of the other parts of the organization. For example, the FDIC was required to absorb its temporary sister organization, the Resolution Trust Corporation (RTC), as part of the latter's sunset legislation. At the time the two organizations conducted their best practices analysis (see Chapter One), both were changing dramatically. Unfortunately, the legislative mandate driving the analysis was more important than the organizations' readiness. The FDIC and RTC senior leaders were supportive and thoughtful in their approach, but they had only limited control over the scope. Virtually all major processes were compared—a daunting effort for any organization. Further, they had been predetermined to be partners by the legislative oversight committee; they could not look outside their organizations' boundaries. These requirements left them little flexibility, even when it was warranted. The project leaders should have been given greater latitude in methods and in identifying best practices. Successful implementation was put at risk.

A much more favorable environment existed in West Virginia. Department heads participated in the state government's benchmarking training conducted by Coopers & Lybrand, so they understood the methodology and purpose before selecting the process to benchmark. The state agencies were ready to benchmark because the Inspire Initiative, the plan to improve state services, had them focus on customers, process improvement, and measurement. The senior leaders solicited ideas from many employees in the state government before selecting the process for benchmarking.

Senior leaders should have a hand in selecting the benchmarking partners and when possible participate in the site visits. The benchmarking team presented a list of potential partners to the city manager in Reno and to senior leaders in Salt Lake City. In both cases these leaders highly endorsed the choices. More important, the benchmarking team, composed of people from both cities, perceived the enthusiasm and support of leaders in the two cities, and team members began thinking of the site visits as an adventure.

Finally, senior leaders must be involved in sustaining the desired changes. When the team returns from the site visit and proposes changes, leaders must think strategically and ensure that steps taken in the short term will contribute to long-term success.

Customers and Stakeholders

A readiness assessment considers not only the agency's readiness but also that of customers and other stakeholders, who might resist changes in areas that are proposed for benchmarking. Team members are better off knowing about these sensitive areas sooner rather than later. Salt Lake City learned this lesson belatedly. The city offers an annual special collection of virtually any solid waste material, including concrete, construction debris, and refrigerators, at a very low cost to citizens. City officials wanted to undertake a benchmarking study to discover ways other cities had found to balance customer expectations of this service with its true costs. Constituents became quite vocal when the mayor and council discussed two alternatives: reducing services while maintaining the current charge to constituents; and maintaining the current level of services at a higher fee. For several reasons, including the public's strong desire for continuing the current service levels at the current price, the benchmarking study was halted about halfway through.

Customers and stakeholders may also be helpful in providing insight into measures they would like to see. Not long ago the FDIC's Training and Consulting Service Branch was poised to design a customer survey to be used for internal benchmarking. The goal was admirable: to ask its customers how it was performing. Working with the iKon Group, the FDIC conducted focus groups and discovered five critical points of contact for its customers. Survey questions were then designed to measure and monitor the FDIC's performance at these points. Without the customers' input, the survey may have focused on areas that were less important to customers, and the benchmarking would have been less meaningful in the long run.

The Benchmarking Champion

The benchmarking champion is a senior leader who becomes the strongest advocate for the benchmarking project and thus plays a pivotal role in its success. Because of his or her position as a senior leader, the champion is expected to

- Understand the external political factors and seek support of the benchmarking project to ensure its success
- Ensure that adequate and accurate resources are dedicated to the project
- Encourage the project coordinator and team members
- Serve as a liaison between the internal and external benchmarking participants and senior managers
- Monitor the progress of the project and provide guidance when necessary
- Interpret results from a strategic and political perspective
- Design and promote the organizational change necessary to implement the actions designed to bring improvement

The champion gives strength and continuity to the project. It is the champion, or the group that fills that role, who can make or break a project. As we noted earlier, the strategy in West Virginia was to incorporate the champion role into an oversight team, whose job was to ensure that resources were allocated to the project, that the work team stayed focused, and that the process ran smoothly. But in one of the projects, One-Stop Business Registration, the oversight team was occasionally an impediment to progress because it took on a more supervisory role, so the benchmarking team was not always empowered to move ahead.

The champion serves as a catalyst for propelling the project forward. Especially for a first benchmarking project, the champion must actively seek feedback from teams and contribute thoughts and insights on the site visit. The champion's greatest responsibility surfaces toward the end of the project, when he or she takes on the role of change agent, acting on recommendations and looking for ways to reinforce success.

Early in the project, the champion frequently identifies a project coordinator, who works closely with the champion and is the key point of contact for team members and stakeholders. The coordinator, who must understand the fundamentals of the benchmarking methodology, also serves these additional functions:

- Identifying others who may be appropriate participants in applying the benchmarking methods
- Coordinating the data collection
- Answering basic questions, such as why the project is important, when it should be undertaken, and where the team should meet
- Coordinating any site visits
- Interacting with benchmarking partners as more complex questions arise
- Ensuring that data collection is completed in a timely and accurate manner

Process Owners

The people most familiar with the process can provide valuable answers to some of the questions raised in previous chapters: Does the process have improvement potential? Where does it move across departments? What data suggest that the customer is concerned about this process? What attempts have been made to improve the process in the past? Did they succeed or fail?

The process owners may contribute the greatest amount of the quantitative information that will be used to gain the support of politicians and to make a final selection. For example, Salt Lake City's measurement team was sufficiently familiar with the customer referral process to select it for benchmarking, but did not have many details. The process participants and owners joined the project when the initial training was delivered. This early participation was important. The process owners provided the details that were needed and at the same time acquired an understanding of the methodology and the goals of the project. In West Virginia, state agencies had been searching for a one-stop business registration process for nine years before benchmarking began. Subsequently employees from each of the five agencies that would be affected by the registration form joined the benchmarking team, ensuring that their ownership and motivation were strong.

Excluding process owners can jeopardize the benchmarking project. In Salt Lake City, the benchmarking of the special collection of solid waste did not go smoothly, as the customer referral project did. An early sign of problems was that the employees involved in the special collections of solid waste did not attend the first day of benchmarking training because of a communication mix-up. Although they came for the second day of training, enthusiasm had waned, and a sense of playing catch-up had developed. Ultimately the project suffered from delays and a lack of a clear focus, and the benchmarking methodology was abandoned. Later a survey of fifteen cities was conducted, and it yielded solid information that contributed to several decisions about solid waste collection, but this approach was very distant from the benchmarking methodology.

Administrative, Budget, and Audit Staff

Public sector budgetary challenges may warrant the involvement of internal fiscal analysts. They can explain how to measure costs or determine how resource intensive processes are—invaluable information for selection criteria. A human resources director may be able to offer advice on how to anticipate and deal in advance with the impact of improvement actions. (Training, for example, may be necessary if technology is introduced or employees are moved elsewhere.) Internal auditors are likely to have considerable information about the operation of the process, historical challenges and successes, and legal or regulatory requirements.

The benchmarking training delivered in Salt Lake City included representatives from the mayor's office, the office of the city council, the budget office, and the utilities, airport, and information resources areas. Participants from the budget and city council offices raised excellent questions about measurements and costs that helped the team members determine how to measure the process.

Team Members

The team members may be the last group to get involved in the benchmarking project. At least one or two are likely to be among the process owners who contributed information and data as selection criteria, but other team members will need to be chosen. This is when an agency's prior experience with quality management or reengineering pays off, because the guidelines for members of a quality improvement team are virtually identical to those for a benchmarking team. Team members should be drawn from various steps in the overall process. For example, a social services benchmarking team should at least include a caseworker, an administrative person, and perhaps a representative from the information systems area. A team should consist of between five and nine members. With fewer members the agency risks focusing on too narrow a portion of the process, and with more the team process itself becomes cumbersome. When did you last try to coordinate the schedules of ten people? If the project is very large, multiple teams may be helpful. Several teams may be formed to benchmark different aspects of the process, and team members may participate in varying degrees at various points. Following are some guidelines to keep in mind when working with team members:

Be sure to provide advance notice of their participation. We once facilitated a process definition session where individuals were notified that very day of the need for their contribution.

Give team members adequate training. They will perform better if they fully understand the overall benchmarking steps; the objectives, risks, and chances of success; and where and how they will contribute to the effort. In West Virginia, project team members became the actual expediters of the benchmarking process, so it was imperative that they receive the same benchmarking training as upper-management personnel. This training, coupled with a time line and guidance provided by the consultant and focus provided by the oversight teams, ensured that the project teams had the preparation and skills necessary to begin. In Salt Lake City the consultant took the teams through a two-day training session, first focusing on benchmarking concepts in general, then covering application of the process at home. In addition, the consultant was available to the teams for follow-up questions and issues and was the facilitator for all subsequent meetings.

Communicate expectations regarding the time commitment. The project coordinator and champion should pave the way by notifying leaders in the agency that this project will require resources, especially staff time. Be sure to shift workloads when appropriate.

Give team members adequate access to the consultant. The role of the consultant is crucial in the first stages of benchmarking. In West

Virginia the benchmarking consultant had been hired to conduct just the initial three-day training session, but when it turned out the consultant's services would be needed for a longer period of time, a new contract had to be drawn up. While the contract was being prepared, there was a period of about a month when the teams did not have access to the consultant. The Measuring Customer Satisfaction team, in particular, found it troublesome to be without guidance during the crucial first few weeks of benchmarking application.

The consultant should be available and involved in the benchmarking project from beginning to end. If this is not possible, then teams should consider working with a knowledgeable mentor who can shepherd them through the problems.

Chapter Seven

Finding a Best Practice Partner

In August 1994 the Parks and Recreation Department in Arlington, Texas, selected four functions to benchmark: customer complaints, telephone etiquette, desk etiquette, and staff training. Its chosen partners were Marriott Corporation, North Vancouver Parks and Recreation Department, Las Colinas Sports Club, BT Miller, the Worthington Hotel, and the Fort Worth Zoo (Heller, 1994, p. 1). When initiating its benchmarking study, the Milwaukee Fire Department chose to follow in the footsteps of Portland, Oregon. The fire department of Lynchburg, Virginia, conducted its comparisons with seven other cities: Charlotte, North Carolina; Sacramento, California; Kansas City, Missouri; Cincinnati, Ohio; Denver, Colorado; Portland, Oregon; and Seattle, Washington (Public Management Group, *Program Performance,* n.d., p. 8).

Salt Lake City and Reno began their forays into benchmarking by comparing themselves solely with each other; they then extended their searches in tandem, finding Charlotte and Seattle along the way. West Virginia's three benchmarking projects began with internal agency assessments as well; their teams eventually selected a diverse array of partners from both the private and public sectors.

The search for benchmarking partners can seem daunting, and an organization brave enough to go outside its field will find a bewildering array of government agencies, units, entities, departments, and divisions—never mind the myriad of private corporations—to consider. It has to determine where the search begins, the extent of the search (for example, should it stretch as far as other countries?), and how it will assemble a list of partners, then pare that list down to the perfect few.

Overall Approach to Partner Selection

The overall approach to partner selection begins by building a database of the team's personal knowledge of potential partners that captures the key reasons why each name goes on the list (Weisendanger, 1993). For example, someone in the agency may have read an article that described a good practice, or may know someone high in the organization, or have heard that the organization uses good performance measures.

Virtually every potential partner identified goes on the initial list, and none should be eliminated before full consideration. This list is a filter, and you will need a large number of possibilities to ensure that only the best reach the final list.

Forget about partner categories. Many authors use the terms *competitive* and *industry* to classify the type of partners to pursue, but we have found these terms, along with *public, private,* and *nonprofit,* to be far less important than the selection criteria developed. The process for selecting partners is more critical than putting the partners into artificial categories.

Involve others in getting ideas for partners. Now is the time to tap personal or professional acquaintances, including customers and politicians, to get their ideas on who might be a good benchmarking partner. A brief description of the process targeted for benchmarking will prompt their ideas.

In a small organization that plans to use only internal partners, in-depth research may not be necessary. Internal partners are physically close and therefore convenient to consult, and they are knowledgeable about the overall organization. Using internal partners may be the best approach when the team is new to benchmarking or when other constraints limit the search. Project leaders should query in-house managers and employees about better practices in other divisions. Experienced managers and employees are an excellent source of reliable and accurate information, so their opinions and ideas are useful for gathering an initial list of departmental partners. Additionally, previously issued technical, monthly, or status reports can be reviewed for hints, insights, or remarks relevant to process improvement.

The Research Process

With the growing popularity of benchmarking, best practice organizations have become reluctant to work with any but the most serious and sincere partners. Benchmarking teams that do their homework—demonstrating that they have already invested in learning about the process and a prospective partner—will impress potential candidates and make them more receptive to collaboration. Preliminary research is important because it establishes the foundation on which a relationship will be built. If the benchmarking team members appear knowledgeable and informed, they will be much better received than a team that stumbles in its pitch when the potential partner asks questions about the project. An agency may not have a second chance to make a favorable first impression.

The sources of information about good potential benchmarking partners are plentiful and inexpensive, but effort is needed to find them. The research will broaden and deepen the benchmarking team's understanding, but team members should expect that the research will raise more questions than it supplies answers. The answers will come as the project unfolds.

We have identified four major sources of information about benchmarking partners: the literature, personal contacts, benchmarking databases, and other third-party services.

The Literature

Libraries, professional organizations and associations, government documents, and newsletters are among the reliable sources of literature about benchmarking and potential benchmarking partners.

A few questions will help to focus the literature search—for example:

- Who has been recognized for improving customer service?
- What technologies are useful to this process?

- What organization has identified innovative ways to handle this process?

Once a few questions are formulated, a trip to the library is in order. Local universities or colleges may be especially helpful for locating a wide range of written materials and multimedia sources.

State or local oversight commissions, national watchdog groups, and professional associations may publish newsletters or reports relevant to the topic. For example, possible sources for fire departments or EMS groups are the International Association of Fire Chiefs and the National Fire Academy. Police chiefs can locate successful community policing efforts through their national association and industry journals, which often feature articles exploring new methods of service delivery.

Organizations that catch the interest of a researcher should be added to the list of potential partners, along with a brief explanation for their selection. Researchers may collect several articles about the same best practice or high-performing organization, confirming that it should be on the list.

Personal Contacts

Now is the time for the benchmarking team to draw on its wide network of professional and personal acquaintances and contacts from a number of groups.

Key Customers or Stakeholders

Customers may have links to people in the community or other government agencies that may be good partners. The organization's customers may include corporations or associations familiar with benchmarking or partnering. If customers or stakeholders have participated in earlier steps of the project, their ideas may already have been gathered. In fact, there is a distinct possibility that potential partners are already customers of or stakeholders in the agency.

Acquaintances from Professional Conferences

Names can be gleaned from business cards collected over the years at professional conferences. Those who attend conferences are generally interested in networking and staying current in their fields and will be flattered by a call for assistance. These colleagues may provide names or ideas worth pursuing.

Elected or Appointed Officials

Many politicians are looking for innovative ways to improve government, thereby increasing their chances of reelection or reappointment. They may have ideas on how to improve various processes. In many instances, an idea that a politician offers originated elsewhere. Tracking down the source of the idea may reveal a promising partner.

Counterparts in Other Jurisdictions

Counterparts in another city, state, or federal agency may have ideas that are worthwhile to the entire benchmarking project, including possibilities for potential partners. They may express a strong interest in hearing from the benchmarking team on completion of the project, because they too are looking for best practices.

Experts in the Field

Experts in the industry—officers in associations, university professors, trade analysts, consultants, or reporters for relevant journals—will be flattered by the interest and should enthusiastically contribute material to projects because the publicity benefits them as well. In the course of talking with experts, the benchmarking team should seek any studies that have not been published or are on the verge of being published. The information in these reports, usually on the cutting edge of the topic, will give the organization an advantage over others.

Existing Research

Consider approaching people who have already done the legwork. For example, when assembling their collection of articles, "Focus on the Best," Barrett and Greene (1993) interviewed dozens of experts—including city managers, mayors, budget directors, and program leaders—and plowed through stacks of statistics and documents in order to write about cities that truly lead the pack in certain urban issues. Any team searching for benchmarking partners should consider tapping writers for their reports and supporting documentation. Why conduct a search that somebody else has already done?

Benchmarking Databases

Computer technology has expedited the search for partners and best practices. Numerous databases are easily accessible, but they frequently contain an overwhelming amount of information, so expect to spend some time sorting through them. Capitalize on the masses of data that other agencies and interest groups have been accumulating and analyzing for years. The Arlington County Fire Department identified its partners from a database maintained by Phoenix, Arizona, which lists over two hundred municipalities providing fire and EMS services categorized by population, square mileage, and density (Plaugher, 1995).

Membership privileges in professional, trade, and industry associations frequently include access to data that the association tracks and has on file. The American Productivity and Quality Center (APQC), for example, provides a host of services related to benchmarking and best practices. Through its International Benchmarking Clearinghouse, the center advises, makes referrals, and offers technical assistance, an on-line network with access to a best practices database, topic-focused conferences, training, publications, and videos. APQC will research a topic, link the requesting organization with industry and professional associations, identify functions for the benchmarking team to work on first, train the team in the process, and analyze data. It will also conduct a complete benchmarking study for organizations that cannot devote the necessary staff and resources to such a study. However, APQC provides this service only to registered members and at significant cost.

As of October 1994, APQC was not collecting performance measurements or metrics in specific industries, though some are included in their best practices data. APQC will, however, make referrals to sources of quantitative information, and it keeps a list of organizations that are the best in certain functions, which benchmarkers can tap for potential partners. The center's database includes abstracts describing successful and innovative practices (what APQC calls "best practices"); a benchmark studies registry to link firms that have conducted or are currently conducting the same search; benchmarking documents, such as surveys and process maps; and listings of additional sources, such as research reports, libraries, consultants, and other databases. APQC lists about thirty agencies and divisions of the federal government as members (American Productivity and Quality Center, n.d., pp. 1–8).

The American Society for Quality Control (ASQC) has created The Benchmarking Exchange (TBE), a dial-up electronic bulletin board with three main options for benchmarkers: they can post notes to solicit partners, search a best practices database to find journal citations of organizations identified as having best practices in selected activities, and search a directory of corporations that provide information to those seeking partners ("Benchmarking Code of Conduct," 1994, p. 15).

The Alliance for Redesigning Government, a NAPA subcommittee, has established the Public Innovators Information Cooperative network (National Academy of Public Administration, *Public Innovators Information Cooperative,* n.d., p. 1). The cooperative has gone on-line with a World Wide Web database, which currently has fourteen categories of case studies, articles, summaries, reports, and contacts. The alliance's home page is not limited to benchmarking and best practices, however. The database, which has a broader purpose of disseminating ideas and connecting public administrators, accepts submissions on government reform of any kind and at any level. Benchmarkers seeking assistance and information will have to search through the available topics (Scully, 1995).

The Internet already contains several sources of additional information about benchmarking and partnering. Specialized chat groups, home pages, and other corners of the Web are growing in numbers every day. An experienced surfer should periodically scan the Net for relevant information.

Other Third-Party Services

Dozens of external services provide assistance in the search for benchmarking partners. Most of them charge a fee, either for membership or for consulting. The Public Sector Network (PSN), a technical committee of the ASQC, was founded to help public sector agencies provide useful services to citizens by promoting the development, use, and documentation of quality management "and to advance a systems approach to the public sector that will foster collaboration between federal, state, and local governments" *(Public Sector Network News,* 1994, p. 1). The founders of PSN had noted that improvement initiatives were popping up all over, but practicing agencies had little or no communication with each other. PSN's focus is not to assist localities with benchmarking and best practices implementation; rather, it has designated itself a primary source of information on best practices in government, an organizer of conferences and seminars, a liaison for fostering intergovernmental cooperation, and a clearinghouse for case studies, success stories, and examples (p. 1). Begun in the summer of 1994, PSN looks promising but could take a few years to become truly effective.

In response to the profusion of performance measurement tools and reference materials, the Innovation Group developed the Standard Reporting of Performance Measures (SRPM), a shared database for cities and counties nationwide to facilitate the collection and reporting of data ("Innovation Group's Standard Reporting of Performance Measures," n.d.) In addition to its performance measurement data, each community and program submits a profile to the SRPM via disk and hard copy. One hundred and thirty-five member localities now share standardized performance measures with each other, thereby facilitating partnering and benchmarking.

The Innovation Group developed standardized reporting forms used to analyze data for forty-four service areas common to local governments, including animal control, building inspection, fire and police services, planning and zoning, library services, and parks and grounds. For each program included, there are two input, two output, two efficiency, and two effectiveness measures. (See Table 7.1 for sample measures or refer to Chapter One for a discussion of performance measures.) This tool allows participants to identify their strong and weak areas in comparison with others as well as with recognized best practice jurisdictions. The forms will not analyze data, identify partners, or calculate performance gaps; they only supply the necessary information. Each participant is free to interpret the data, identify best practices, and contact the relevant jurisdictions ("Innovation Group's Standard Reporting of Performance Measures," n.d.).

Table 7.1. Sample Generic Measures.

Inputs	Outputs	Efficiency	Effectiveness
Number of full-time equivalents	Number of service requests fulfilled	Number of requests per full-time equivalents	Average time required to fulfill request
Operating budget	Number of claims processed	Dollars spent per claim	Numbers of claims processed correctly on initial attempt

Best practices and benchmarking services, consultants, and databases may sound like simple, elegant solutions, but the utility and value of these services are finite and deserve thorough evaluation. Employing experts has advantages and disadvantages. On the positive side, consultants have a breadth of experience from leading other organizations in benchmarking efforts. They play the role of the reliable guide who speaks the native tongue, knows the safest routes, and lends a sense of security to the exploration team. Good consultants provide more than just theoretical training; they can help in researching a partner, are generous with what they know, and can troubleshoot when the inevitable snags in the process come along. West Virginia, for example, had no internal personnel with sufficient expertise in benchmarking, so the state hired a Big Six consulting firm to facilitate its benchmarking process. Without exception, the three benchmarking teams in West Virginia spoke highly of their relationship with the consultant.

Consultants also act as a neutral third party. With performance improvement their sole goal, they can assist in the selection of partners, make the initial contacts, follow up on those contacts, and organize and plan site visits from an objective standpoint. Unlike the members of the benchmarking team, consultants are not stakeholders in the project; they can remain more objective in the pursuit of best practices. A benchmarking partner is more likely to be realistic about what it can actually do for the benchmarking organization if it is dealing with a third party; it is less likely to be overwhelmed by the flattery of a public agency and make promises it cannot keep.

Hiring a consultant is not necessarily the best choice for all organizations. Thus far, few consultants have guided public sector entities through the benchmarking maze. Most have assisted only private corporations in such endeavors. Additionally, any organization will learn more about itself and its professional area by conducting the exercise internally. Contracting the work out means the organization will forgo some of the inherent benefits of a best practices effort. Instead, those benefits will be rerouted to the consultant, increasing his or her knowledge, know-how, database, and present value. If done in-house, researching and locating potential partners will advance the buy-in process for all individuals and groups within the organization. Benchmarkers considering hiring an outside source to direct or assist in the project should be aware of the trade-off between time and knowledge and should evaluate their organization's needs accordingly.

Narrowing the List of Potential Partners

Once potential partners are consolidated into a single list, the process of narrowing the field begins. We emphasize that this is a process because there are many aspects to consider about partners and no magical formula for their selection. The perfect partner for one agency may not be right for a different agency. We cannot make the choice for you but can only describe how to reach a satisfactory answer.

Step One: Set Aside the Partner List

Team members will be tempted to talk about which organizations are on the list and why. They may already be leaning toward and enthusiastically discussing a handful of names on the list and may have prematurely concluded that certain partners must have the solution to the problem. This is the point at which a strong leader or facilitator must step in to ensure that the team carefully establishes selection criteria. Prematurely choosing partners may mean that the team overlooks a golden opportunity to identify a best practice more fitting to its environment.

Step Two: Establish Criteria for Making Partner Selection

Filtering hundreds of potential partners through the decision-making process is impossible without prerequisites or criteria. But criteria in themselves can number in the thousands—everything from daytime population to average inches of annual snowfall—so it is important to choose them carefully. Setting limits or boundaries around the field of choices puts everybody on the project team in the same frame of mind, ensures shared expectations, and reduces the chances of misinterpretation and last-minute surprises.

It would be impossible to list all of the possible criteria, so we have chosen a few categories worthy of any team's consideration. Review this list, then develop your own criteria. Start by answering the question, What are the characteristics desired in a partner?

- Demonstrated performance
- Work processes
- Mission
- Professional field
- Number of functions to be benchmarked
- Performance measures
- Type of government
- Demographics
- Geographic location
- Size of partner organization
- Technology

Demonstrated Performance

The best practice criteria identified in Chapter One can be used as a guide to help determine how clearly a potential partner has demonstrated that it has a best practice.

Work Processes

Because an organization's readiness should influence the selection criteria, the desired similarities or differences in a partner should be closely examined. As discussed in Chapter Three, the simplest benchmarking project is one that directly compares a particular function or process to virtually the same process or function in another organization. This method is safe and reliable because the benchmarking organization is almost ensured that the practices chosen for importing will map directly and easily. Although there may be no breakthrough innovations, incremental improvement through better practices is a reasonable choice. We recommend that you review the discussion on readiness in Chapter Three. An agency that is new to benchmarking or has a low readiness for other reasons will want to select a partner that is similar.

Starting off in familiar territory lends a feeling of security and reduces the risk of failure. This safe approach also may be especially attractive to a unit with highly specialized services. For example, the fire and EMS department of Lynchburg, Virginia, chose to benchmark similar departments in three Virginia localities and six other cities, including Greensboro, North Carolina; Salem, Oregon; and Springfield, Ohio (Public Management Group, *Fire/EMS Benchmarks*, n.d., p. 3). The fire department of Arlington County, Virginia, sent reconnaissance teams to Phoenix, Arizona, and has established a solid relationship with the fire department there (Barvenik and Davis, 1995).

The more experienced and proficient an organization becomes at importing best practices, however, the better able it is to search for partners that are less similar to itself. Partnering with diverse organizations lends itself to a blending of core competencies and capabilities with complementary strengths of the outside partner, thereby strengthening the benchmarking organization's overall capability, speed, and flexibility (National Institute of Standards and Technology, 1995, p. 4).

A natural progression of partnering accompanies benchmarking maturation. For instance, the first partner that the Arlington, Texas, recreation department selected did not connect well with the department's operation (Heller, 1994, p. 10). The department recommended that subsequent benchmarking studies focus on organizations with more similar missions or on other parks and recreation agencies. Because this was its first foray into benchmarking, the department team did not have the experience or sophistication to use effectively the information garnered from dramatically different partners.

In an interview with us, the team leader from West Virginia's Employee Training project emphasized the importance of using selection criteria as a guide, not as a crutch or limitation. She cited an example of a cable company that had benchmarked with a company that produced noodles. The products were quite different, but the manufacturing processes were much the same. The criteria helped the team understand the important similarities and avoid summarily rejecting a potential partner. This analogy was helpful to the Employee Training team, whose mandate was to locate a good, effective process for delivering training.

Mission

A county department of social services that is benchmarking information systems in the state highway patrol may find differences between the mission and environment of the two organizations that may lead to complications that it would not have encountered had it benchmarked a federal social services information system or that of another county.

Number of Functions to Be Benchmarked

An agency that is overhauling several activities simultaneously may seek a partner that is very similar. Whether one internal team is handling all the processes or a separate team has been established for each process to be benchmarked will have a bearing on partner selection criteria.

Performance Measures

Research has probably given the benchmarking team a sense of what measures a potential partner is using to monitor performance. The team should consider whether these measures seem appropriate or appealing, whether they correspond to the expectations of the agency's customers, whether the agency has comparable measures or indicators, and whether the measures cover a wide range of performance, such as timeliness, efficiency, outcome, or outputs.

An agency may prefer to select all partners from a common database, such as the Innovation Group's SRPM. As participants in the database, these organizations have collected and reported measures in a similar or consistent fashion.

Type of Government

It may be important that a partner represent a particular form of government. Salt Lake City and Reno each preferred a city that had a similar form of government to theirs. Thus they selected Charlotte (council-manager) and Seattle (strong mayor-council) as their partners. An agency's customers, elected leaders, or oversight committees may be more convinced of the potential for improvement if a partner operates under the same form of government in the same professional sector. For example, the Florida Department of Insurance may wish to compare itself with the Minnesota Department of Insurance rather than the Allstate Insurance Agency. We remind you, though, that truly breakthrough improvements typically come from more diverse comparisons. Each agency's team is in the best position to determine how far from the organization it should venture.

Agencies can pinpoint partners based on the organization of services, such as centralized or decentralized. When Salt Lake City and Reno set about benchmarking other entities, both had a preliminary idea of the direction in which they wanted to go. They targeted similar-sized cities where the administration had established a centralized system for receiving and handling customer complaints and requests for information, thereby eliminating localities that did not have the activity organized in such a fashion.

Demographics

Characteristics of the jurisdiction, such as unemployment rate, average income and years of education, major growth industries, and number of new housing developments may influence partner selection. Other important considerations may be urban versus rural environment, average age, family size, and mode of transportation. The agency should select only the demographics that are relevant to the project.

Geographic Location

Even regional weather patterns can influence partner selection. Snow removal, pothole repairs, and storm water drainage may be unique to a particular geographic location. The location of a partner therefore might weigh heavily on selection criteria. Also, if the travel allowance for the project is limited, one possibility to explore is the trade-off between having several team members visit a partner that is nearby versus having one or two members visit a partner that is farther away and therefore more expensive to get to.

Size of Partner Organization

The benchmarking team needs to determine how many people they are willing to deal with to review and adopt a practice. In large organizations, a process may wind its way through several divisions and a hundred individuals, so the team must be sufficiently organized to deal with those numbers. Other considerations are whether the team will feel more secure working with partners that have a limited number of customers. An organization benchmarking a state department of taxation must be prepared to deal with a customer count in the millions, whereas a county motor pool may serve only a few hundred customers.

The size of the partner's budget may be another factor influencing the decision. Again, if your annual allotment is $3.4 million and the prospective partner's is $14 million, this discrepancy may explain why the partner has an untouchable caliber of service.

Technology

Technology is likely to be an important aspect of any benchmarking endeavor. This criterion was very important to Salt Lake City and Reno because both were only interested in finding partners that used advanced technology to automate their customer referral process.

In a hypothetical scenario, if your unit manages a particular activity using forms and files, you probably want to benchmark only agencies that run the activity electronically. Likewise, if the process you are benchmarking is interdepartmental employee communication and your organization currently uses telephone voice mail, you may want to choose only partners that have electronic mail systems. Partners may also be designated on the basis of their use of cellular phones, laptop computers, CD-ROMs, or the presence of the World Wide Web, advanced sanitation systems, automated wastewater treatment facilities, and so forth. In other words, your organization will consider only organizations that successfully employ the cutting-edge mechanisms to conduct or manage a function similar to yours. In this situation, we recommend that at least one permanent team member be a specialist in the technology you believe is important to the benchmarked subject.

The list of selection criteria deserves careful review and thoughtful discussion, with all team members clear as to what they want the criteria to reveal. For example, if team members agree that size is important, what do they mean by size—number of employees, total dollars in the budget, number of clients served, or something else? Once size is defined, a decision must be made as to the optimum partner size—larger, smaller, or comparable to the benchmarking organization?

Step Three: Apply the Criteria

This step can range from the simple to the complex. Some criteria may be mandatory for a partner to meet. For example, an agency benchmarking snow removal must find a partner in an area that receives significant amounts of snow.

The process starts with the required criteria, the first eliminations being the potential partners that do not meet them. A useful tool is a matrix check sheet, with the criteria listed on the horizontal axis and the potential partners on the vertical axis. Place a check in the organization's block if it meets the criterion.

You probably need to assign numeric values to the criteria to give more weight to more critical items. For example, a potential partner may receive ten points for having a similar process and only two points for similar demographics. Assign the appropriate points to each partner, total the amount, and rank eligible organizations in descending order.

You can also rate each candidate partner on a scale, for example, of one to five, on how well it meets each criterion and then tally the overall scores. This is a more complex rating system. The team will have several chances to discuss which potential partners are eliminated after applying a scale.

Step Four: Narrow the List

Do not expect the ideal partner to surface the first time you apply the criteria. In fact, this is an iterative process of making a cut, reducing the list, and reexamining the remainder in the light of the established criteria or additional criteria. Typically some natural breaks in data will occur. If someone on the team strongly opposes dropping a potential partner, by all means retain it. In the early stages of partner selection, it is better to err on the side of inclusion than exclusion. Eventually partners that best suit the agency's situation and goals will emerge.

Determining the Number of Partners

What is the optimum number of partners? A list of more than thirty organizations to start with shows that the team did a good job of researching potential partners. Using the criteria will usually reduce the list to about ten. If the initial pool started with ten, the goal here should be to reduce it to five.

Several additional considerations are important before proceeding with the selection of partners. Is the goal to seek only a few extraordinary partners or a large cross section of the sector? Logically more partners mean more effort on the benchmarker's part. We usually recommend that public sector organizations on their first benchmarking expedition limit their partners to three or fewer if they plan to conduct site visits. Each agency has to decide on its own optimum number because even the experts disagree on the appropriate number of partners.

Bruder and Gray (1994) believe that having fewer than four partners eliminates a variety of ideas, statistical significance, and the quantity of useful data, whereas having as many as sixteen produces a lot of information of little value. They suggest that six is the happy medium to aim for, and then give a warning not to choose agencies just because their information is readily available. The hard work of digging for unpublicized data should yield helpful information and improve the partner dossier.

West Virginia's Employee Training project team began with a list of over thirty companies and agencies. Through follow-up research that entailed calling prospective partners with questions based on their selection criteria, team members reduced the list to twenty, then to twelve, and finally to ten. Working with an outside statistician, they drew up a partner questionnaire that could be assessed both quantitatively and qualitatively. It contained similar questions to those used in the baseline questionnaire but also included a request for more open-ended, anecdotal information, asking the partners to respond on a separate sheet of paper with narratives that focused on process. The team anticipated that feedback from the partner questionnaire would narrow the field even further. They ended up with seven partners in a process that was well researched, informed, and efficient.

Choosing Between a Public Sector and a Private Sector Partner

Public agencies may make an incorrect assumption that a private sector partner is preferable. They may reason that private companies are motivated by profits to improve their performance and that benchmarking is more prevalent in the private sector. Unless an agency has a particular need to select one or the other, however, this factor should not be given undue weight. Certainly it should already have been considered in the discussions to determine how similar or dissimilar a partner should be and in what dimensions. Beware of becoming sidetracked with discussions about private versus public unless that issue directly relates to the established criteria. If it is a contentious issue, select a partner from each sector.

West Virginia's One-Stop Business Registration project team considered private sector companies but ultimately rejected them. The team's selection criteria, which were fairly specific because of technological concerns, forced the team to consider only public agencies with strong technical networking capabilities and diverse functions, something the private sector companies they researched did not have.

Salt Lake City and Reno considered looking to the private sector for benchmarking partners. But because this was the team's first venture in benchmarking, their consultant advised that they would have a greater chance for success by working exclusively with other public sector agencies.

Deciding on a Time Frame

What is the time frame for the project—turnaround in two months or a two-year, in-depth project? Must there be improvement by a deadline, or can the project be completed at its own pace? Carla O'Dell of the IIL recently noted that benchmarking exercises in the private sector that in the past required six to twelve months to complete have been reengineered themselves and now take only two to four months (International Institute for Learning, 1995a, p. 12). An agency with an exceptional amount of support, guidance, or clarity of goals may need less time. The number of partners selected may be determined by the project's time line.

All of these and numerous additional issues are factored into partner selection. Recognize that this is an iterative process that deserves time and thoughtful consideration. The final decision should be driven less by a number and more by the characteristics identified as important in a partner. Once the team reaches agreement on the potential partner list, it moves into planning for the initial contact.

Just because those assigned to the task have located a partner that fits the criteria does not mean the potential partner will automatically accept this role. A request for cooperation could be denied for a number of reasons or simply because the target organization does not buy into benchmarking. For instance, the target partner could be going through financial or personnel upheaval, changes in political leadership, reorganization of career senior management, a corporate takeover, or a period of reengineering and thus cannot spare the time or resources to cooperate as a partner. Perhaps the organization is being investigated for wrongdoing, fraud, or corruption. The inquiry to determine a potential partner's interest requires careful timing.

What can you do to ensure that partnering expectations will not be dashed against the rocks of circumstance and poor timing? How will you structure your inquiry and sell the partner on your organization? Before anyone makes a move on a partner, give some thought to the first contact with that organization.

Planning for the Initial Contact

Once the benchmarking team has narrowed the list considerably and is ready to make the first request, it needs to spend a little time coordinating the contacts. Here are a few issues the team should consider.

Making the Initial Contact: Mail or Telephone?

A telephone call to the partner organization can serve as the initial screening. The personal touch is helpful even if the caller is passed to several people before reaching the appropriate person. If the potential partner was identified through an article, individuals named in that article may be a good place to start.

We do not usually recommend that the first inquiry be conducted in writing because a letter does not give the caller a chance to sense the reaction or respond to the reader's concerns. Nevertheless, letters can be successful. The fire chief of Arlington County, Virginia, initially approached partners by having a member of the department's benchmarking team, an analyst, write a letter to her equivalent within the chosen municipality. If the team received no response or a negative response, then the chief himself would send a letter directly to his counterpart (Plaugher, 1995). In fact, the benchmarking team has received nothing but positive responses. There are several reasons that the initial letter may have been so successful. The letter's recipient, seeing the signature of an analyst, perhaps did not feel as if she or he was getting a directive from an outside manager. This individual might also have been flattered by the attention and enthused by a request for a site visit. (Site visit techniques will be expanded on in Chapter Eight.) Also a request is more likely to secure the support of a partner's management if it is presented to management by an internal person, not by an unknown quantity.

Identifying Who Will Make the Initial Contact

Should the champion or a high-ranking official make the first contact? A strong hierarchical organization may warrant a call from a high-level official. Should a knowledgeable team member call his or her counterpart? It depends. We do not have a standard answer to these questions because each depends a great deal on the particular situation and the research results. However, team members should use what they know about a potential partner to gain insight on how best to approach it. Also, the team should consider who among its members projects confidence and enthusiasm over the telephone. If someone from the agency has a personal contact with the potential partner's organization, the team should by all means take advantage of it.

Identifying Who Will Serve as Primary Point of Contact

The person making the initial inquiry may or may not be the person who will interact with a partner on a day-to-day basis, so the initial contact should provide the potential partner with the name of someone the partner will speak to regularly. A partner should also designate a single point of contact within its ranks to ensure the smooth flow of information and lessen the chances for misunderstanding. More than one line of communication can give rise to miscommunication, duplicative actions, and confusion that will retard the pace and progress of the benchmarking project. Just as too little communication could lead a partner to question its involvement with the benchmarking organization, too much communication—in the form of incessant questions and unnecessary updates—may annoy the partner's employees to the point of distraction.

A single point of contact or single coordinator becomes crucial when there are multiple site visits. When Salt Lake City and Reno chose to visit Charlotte and Seattle, they preferred that the consultant play the pivotal role of coordinating the visits for everyone in the four cities. Secondary points of contact were designated within the entities being visited. The manager of the Customer Service Center was chosen in Charlotte, as was Seattle's director of the Citizen Service Bureau (Keehley, 1995a, p. 9).

Explaining the Organization's Interest

Benchmarkers should summarize their agency's interest in a prospective partner and how they identified that organization. A team that shows knowledge of the benchmarking method and subject area will demonstrate to the prospective partner that the team is serious in its pursuit of improvement and is willing and eager to do the necessary work.

Explaining the Benefits of Benchmarking to a Potential Public Sector Partner

The caller should be prepared to convey the benefits that will accrue to a public sector partner by participating in the project. As public agencies, the benchmarking team and the potential partner have many things in common, among them the following: (1) culture (virtually all government agencies operate in some sort of fishbowl under the watchful eye of the public, the press, and a number of oversight organizations); (2) human resource management rules, regulations, and laws; (3) functions and processes; (4) citizen clients; (5) budget restrictions; and (6) experiences with unions.

When Salt Lake City became interested in benchmarking, its consultant initiated the idea of cost sharing the benchmarking project with another city. Salt Lake City had identified two areas for improvement: the customer referral process and solid waste management. With those possibilities in mind, the consultant identified over thirty potential partners, finally settling on Reno, which was also interested in improving its customer referral process. Salt Lake City was able to sell the idea of a joint benchmarking effort to Reno by emphasizing similarities in the customer referral process and the excitement of testing a methodology new to the public sector. Another convincing argument Salt Lake City officials used was that both localities could save money by sharing costs and learning from each other, as well as from the outside. Note that this was not a partnering relationship in the typical sense; neither city had a best practice the other wished to emulate. The cities joined forces in order to research best practices together, and their unique bond as public sector agencies made their partnership a viable one.

Explaining the Benefits of Benchmarking to a Potential Private Sector Partner

Private sector organizations may be skeptical that a public sector agency can offer them anything of value in return for their assistance, so the benchmarking team must be able to point out several advantages that may be attractive to a corporate partner. First, public agencies typically have a large and diverse client base, from which a partner may learn how to better serve a broader range of customers. Second, where would a company find a private sector benchmarking partner that has core processes as diverse as police protection, environmental safeguards, and education? To find an abundance of processes and functions in the private sector equal to that of government, the private sector partner would have to seek out huge companies with several divisions. Most private sector firms are too specialized to offer the same wide range of services that a federal, state, or county government can. Third, the public sector frequently embarks on projects on a scale never undertaken in the private sector. For example, the IRS's tax system modernization program was the largest civilian technological modernization in history. A private sector company embarking on a large systems modernization may have much to learn from the IRS about cutting-edge services for millions of people. The more the benchmarking team understands its own agency's strengths and the partner's organization, the better prepared it will be to make these arguments.

Questioning the Potential Partner

After partner interest in the project has been confirmed, the caller can move forward with other questions—for example, Will the subject area be acceptable? Will there be sensitive areas? How about the time frame? Who are the key decision makers who will commit the partner's resources to assisting in the project? Will the organization need a formal or written request for data or information? Will they host a site visit? And so on.

If these inquiries are made by telephone, a worksheet will help to ensure consistency among the calls. Exhibit 7.1 shows a sample worksheet.

The Partnering Process

Partnering is a process in and of itself, and it can often be a very delicate operation, as working with individuals and groups usually is. The benchmarking agency may have to contend with one or several very foreign organizational cultures or acclimate itself to an entirely new way of communicating if that is required to have a productive relationship. For instance, a community recreational center that chooses to benchmark a military outfit must understand that it is temporarily stepping into another world, where communication and interaction between individuals follows a strict set of rules. Benchmarkers need to plan for time for their organization

Exhibit 7.1. Benchmarking Partner Worksheet.

Name of potential partner organization: _____

Primary point of contact: _____

Description of potential partner organization:

_____

_____

_____

Name and description of process(es) to be studied:

_____

_____

_____

Goals and purpose of the study:

_____

_____

_____

Reasons why the organization has been chosen:

_____

_____

_____

Benefits of participation to the partner organization:

_____

_____

_____

Status of the benchmarking project:

_____

_____

_____

Current status of our internal process:

_____

_____

_____

How has the partner documented its process?

_____

_____

_____

Desired time frame/schedule:

_____

_____

_____

Suggestions for format of information exchange:

_____

_____

_____

Sensitive areas/confidentiality requirements:

_____

_____

_____

to adjust; such flexibility does not develop overnight. Careful analysis, research, and sharing will bring any agency closer to choosing an excellent partner.

Examples of Partners

Some case examples of how practitioners find partners can be illuminating. According to William Gay (1992) of the PMG, the Milwaukee Fire Department discovered Portland's smoke detector installation program during a literature search and then chose Portland's low fire-death rate as a standard to which it could aspire. Note that the Milwaukee Fire Department stayed within its industry because that approach suited its goals.

After appointing a benchmarking team of twenty-five practitioners in January 1991, Digital Equipment Corporation (DEC) undertook to find twenty companies to participate in a telephone survey regarding five functions of communication. The team found its targets amid *Fortune*'s "Most Admired Companies" list, an industry journal, and a study conducted by a consulting firm on company reputations. The DEC benchmarking team had set its sights on similar-sized companies that possessed the complexity of the business DEC is in. At the same time, the team wanted to avoid using only computer firms. With these criteria to work with, DEC found a surprising variety of partners: Scott Paper, Campbell's Soup, Whirlpool, Boeing, Hewlett-Packard, and Apple (Weisendanger, 1993, p. 20).

The often-cited example of diverse partners is that of Xerox's benchmarking L. L. Bean for customer satisfaction strategies. The U.S. Bureau of Printing and Engraving, besides providing the nation's money, also sells coins to collectors. It looked far afield, to Lenox China and Black & Decker, for lessons in improving sales operations (National Performance Review, 1995, p. 2).

The International Institute for Learning (1995a, p. 20) provides a hypothetical example in which a video rental store wants to overhaul three processes: inventory management, customer selection, and checkout and return. The store selects partners from audiovisual rental outfits, public libraries, hardware stores that rent tools, costume party renters, and formal wear renters. IIL also refers to the case of an ammunition company that sought to improve the precision shape of its product. It turned to a cosmetics manufacturer for guidance because this partner was world class in producing smooth, shiny containers for its cosmetics that attracted and satisfied customers.

Another good example of diverse comparisons is an airline that wanted to decrease its gate turnaround time. Airplanes that spent less time waiting at the gate would be available for more flights for more customers and would produce greater customer satisfaction. The improvement team took a broad approach and asked themselves, Who are the experts at the quick fix? Their answer: race-car pit crews—a logical partner but as distant a one as there is.

Some benchmarking organizations choose to avoid partnering with their direct competitors. The New York City Transit Authority (NYCTA) examined best practices of other leading multimodal transit authorities; single-modal transit authorities such as Houston and Detroit; foreign transit authorities in Montreal, Tokyo, and Stockholm; and private sector companies, including Federal Express, UPS, and Delta Airlines. Like NYCTA itself, many of these organizations were operating under severe budgetary restrictions created by economic and market pressures (Bruder and Gray, 1994, p. 10). By avoiding taxicab companies, private bus lines, limousine services, or commuter van pools, the transit authority steered clear of partnering with its closest competitors, yet was still successful in making improvement. The Recreation Department of Arlington, Texas, followed the same strategy, forgoing private gyms (with the exception of the Las Colinas Sports Club), recreational associations, and golf and tennis clubs as partners.

In its efforts to identify best practices in telephone service, the NPR sought to work with eight private companies in identifying the methods and techniques the government could employ to close the gap between its performance and that of the best (National Performance Review, 1995, p. 2). Cost management leader Citibank and Malcolm Baldrige Award winners AT&T Universal Card Services and Xerox Corporation were willing to share the factors that make their telephone service excellent and to show federal employees what is necessary to be the best in the business (p. 3).

Chapter Eight

Maximizing the Relationship with Your Partner

The initial contact has been made, and the partner has agreed to provide the requested assistance. The benchmarking team is now at the heart of its project. By paying attention to basic protocols, avoiding a few bad habits, and following some general guidelines for exchanging and collecting information, the team will strengthen its relationship with its partner.

Basic Protocols

Benchmarking necessitates personal interaction, openness, sharing, and a high degree of trust. Respecting the rights and prerogatives of partners is not just good for business; it will also keep the benchmarking organization out of hot water. The following guidelines are basic to the relationship:

- Behave in a straightforward and unequivocal manner.
- Carry out the project with integrity.
- Never misrepresent yourself or your organization.
- Identify all parties who will have access to partner information and the extent of that access. If a partner requests confidentiality, make every effort to honor that request.
- Be sensitive to any potentially touchy issues, and consult your partner on any intended changes to the game plan.

Recognize that all partners have certain ownership rights. Proprietary information includes that "created, acquired, controlled by an organization that has not been published or released without restriction, and that which the organization wishes to maintain confidential" ("Benchmarking Code of Conduct," 1994, p. 17). According to this definition, any kind of information can be proprietary: technical abilities, financial status, product development, and marketing strategy. Avoid headaches and confrontations by requesting and accepting only the types of information that your organization requires to achieve its benchmarking objectives. Acknowledge and accept a partner's definitions, restrictions, and controls with respect to proprietary information.

An agency that is benchmarking a public sector organization must be sensitive to proprietary information. Both Seattle and Charlotte shared with Salt Lake City and Reno several reports and data they wished to remain confidential. A related issue is that a public sector partner may offer materials that it does not know are restricted, such as software developed for its use but copyrighted by the developer.

Respect the personal issues involved in off-the-record comments. There is usually a good reason for such a request, especially in the public sector, where issues may be politically charged. Recognize a partner's sensitivity in areas you may not consider exclusive. The more the partner trusts the benchmarking team members, the more likely they are to hear the truth about what they are benchmarking. Remember to operate with the awareness that private sector partners are not subject to the Freedom of Information Act.

An organization that follows a code of conduct will contribute to efficient, effective, and ethical benchmarking. Many professional organizations have established ethical guidelines for their particular profession, and all benchmarkers should be aware of any unique guidelines recommended by their own. Additionally, the ASQC ("Benchmarking Code of Conduct," 1994) publishes an overall list of ethical guidelines for benchmarking.

All benchmarking teams and partners must establish ground rules that explain how the process will be carried out and establish expectations for all parties' mutual best interest and interactions. Cover the basics, such as the following:

• Maintain a focus on the benchmarking objectives.
• Do not get sidetracked by peripheral issues.

- Be prompt in returning telephone calls (within twenty-four hours).
- Avoid jargon.
- Agree to establish an agenda in advance of telephone calls or meetings.
- Respect proprietary information provided by either the partner or the benchmarking team.

Bad Habits to Avoid

Weisendanger (1993) warns benchmarkers against three types of action: (1) recruiting employees from the partner to obtain information; (2) disclosing information about one partner while working with another partner or in a public arena without the original partner's express consent; and (3) requiring vendors to participate in benchmarking studies as a condition of patronage. Although these actions may not be as relevant to the public organization, a private sector partner may be conscious of them. Assuring the partner that you recognize the potential dangers will convey an awareness and sensitivity important to the partner.

Be careful not to cast any team members in the role of "information taker." Rather, the team should regard the partner relationship as one of information exchange and share the results of data analysis with each partner, or all partners if possible, as well as the results that follow implementation. If partners are learning as much from the project as the benchmarking organization is, they will be more willing to cooperate in the future. Team members who are aware of leads, sources, or ideas being sought by a partner, whether in relation to benchmarking or not, can offer suggestions, imparting to the partner something of value in return for assistance. In other words, all team members should operate with a consistent "How can I return the favor?" frame of mind. Benchmarking teams that interact with partners as if they were building long-term relationships will end up forging lasting associations.

Partners are never perfect. They will likely do a few things that do not make sense to the benchmarking team, and they undoubtedly have areas where they could not overcome some obstacles or hurdles. Even best-in-class organizations need a little encouragement, and a word from the benchmarking organization may go a long way. Charlotte had made great strides in improving its customer service area but continued to face resistance from a few departments. The site visit teams from Salt Lake City and Reno offered no criticism and much sympathy and understanding in regard to the situation.

Finally, "Never let them see you sweat" applies here. Benchmarking teams should never expose partners to any internal controversies, conflict, dissuasion, or discord among people on the team or in the organization. If incidents of this type arise, the team should endeavor not to let them disrupt the schedule of correspondence or affect the nature of the relationship with the host. If the host senses internal strife and wobbling support, the project could peter out before it really begins.

When officials at Digital Equipment Corporation (DEC) were preparing a list of questions to ask their benchmarking partners on public relations functions, planning, and communication, they found themselves in disagreement over how they would answer those questions in terms of DEC itself. They spent several meetings hashing through their own answers to the questions; only when agreement was reached did they use the survey with DEC's partners. Not only did DEC keep its own disagreements private; it came to a better understanding of its own processes by looking at the differing perceptions about public relations held by company members (Weisendanger, 1993, p. 21).

Exchange and Collection of Data

The initial contact provides partners with several important bits of information: the background of the project, reasons for interest in the partner organization, and a proposal indicating how that organization can assist the benchmarking group. Now is the time to summarize this information in writing, along with a written plan for the benchmarking activities that covers the following points:

- Name and brief description of the benchmarking organization
- Name and telephone number of the main point of contact, and names of team members
- Project goals and time line
- Reasons for choosing the partner

- Benefits that accrue to the partner through its participation
- Documentation of the process to be benchmarked
- Terms of confidentiality
- Recommended format for exchanging information

Allow the partner to make comments and suggestions. Once a plan is settled on, the benchmarking team should give the partner as much advance notice as possible when any deviations from the plan become necessary.

Collecting Data Without a Site Visit

Although there are many benefits to a site visit, some organizations seeking better practices, or those that are constrained by time or resources, may choose to collect data without a visit. In this case, the team must select from a number of data collection methods, such as questionnaires or structured telephone interviews, that allow it to work from the home organization. As with any other step in the benchmarking process, careful attention to planning contributes to a more successful process.

Questionnaire Development

An organization that is relying on a questionnaire will need to develop and refine it over several stages to ensure reliability and validity (Ernst & Young, 1993, p. 35). First, the project team members formulate a working draft of key concepts and hypotheses that can be measured. Next, they construct a series of questions applicable to the cultures of the participating organizations. The team members should assess the clarity and conciseness of the developing instrument by putting themselves in the shoes of the partner's employees and customers.

The team members should refine the questions after reflecting on questionnaires they have received to identify which aspects grabbed their attention and made them fun to respond to. Numerous books have been written about survey design and data collection; we recommend adding a few of these books to the organization's reference library and consulting them while developing your survey instrument. Developing a questionnaire is more than brainstorming a list of questions. If no one on the benchmarking team has experience in producing questionnaires, someone from inside or outside the team or organization should be recruited to assist. A poorly worded or ineffective questionnaire can jeopardize a benchmarking project. Someone experienced with survey design will ensure the questionnaire covers all the bases and that the language is appropriate and clear.

Here are some overall suggestions to make the final questionnaire and data gathering more effective:

1. Be clear on the audience. Do not design an instrument for frontline workers and then send it to mid-level managers.
2. Write a brief, smooth introduction.
3. Keep the questionnaire to a few pages.
4. Format the questionnaire for ease of completion. Keep the page uncluttered, and use colors to draw attention to the overall instrument and/or text.
5. If questions cover several topics, write short transitions to each new topic.
6. Make sure that questions flow from the general to the specific, with the most delicate questions coming at the end.
7. Keep questions as simple as possible, and employ a shared vocabulary; use clear, unambiguous phrasing and unbiased language.
8. Provide adequate response alternatives to questions, including "don't know" or "unfamiliar with topic." Avoid stigmatizing lack of knowledge.
9. Give clear instructions.
10. Be sure any scales and descriptors are appropriate to potential responses. For example, do not use a one-to-five scale representing "strongly agree" to "strongly disagree" for a question that requires a yes or no answer.
11. Retest and validate. Before subjecting any partner to questions, expose some coworkers to the instrument, preferably those in positions equivalent to those who will be responding to the questionnaire.
12. To increase the response rate, have an individual or authority within the partnering organization send advance communiqués and follow-up notices within a few days of the actual instrument distribution date.
13. Assure respondents beforehand of complete and continued confidentiality.

14. Use some incentive or reward for those who return a complete survey.

The Employee Training team in West Virginia conducted a baseline survey of roughly sixty-five organizations as a way of collecting best practices. They used pretests to determine the precision and validity of the instrument, and revised it as necessary.

Structured Telephone Interviews

There is no substitute for engaging a partner in a dialogue about the process or activity under study. These discussions may uncover issues not tapped in a questionnaire. Additionally, a conversation conveys a better sense of the less tangible aspects of the partner, such as style and culture. If there is to be no site visit, consider setting up a few structured telephone conversations, with each interviewee asked an identical series of questions that are predetermined by the team. In some instances a conference call in which two or three partner representatives are interviewed simultaneously is helpful. We do not recommend including more than three people because the degree of participation declines dramatically as interviewees are added to the discussion.

Following are guidelines for conducting telephone interviews:

- Establish a timetable and stick to it.
- Agree in advance on agenda items, such as background information and interview questions.
- Fax or mail necessary materials in advance.
- Test the technology in advance if you are using unfamiliar equipment.
- Allow time for the interviewee to ask questions.

Data Collection Monitoring

Once the questionnaires and telephone interviews are under way, one or more team members should monitor data collection to secure the integrity of the information. These individuals should be knowledgeable about the data collection process and available to answer questions regarding all means of data collection being used by the benchmarking organization. Questions will surely arise that will call for further coordination among the data collection points. When Salt Lake City and Reno collected data on incoming telephone calls, they discovered that their predetermined call categories could be interpreted in a variety of ways by the person who answered the call and recorded the data. For example, say that a caller complained that snow had not been removed and requested the street be plowed. Should that call be categorized as a complaint or a request, or both? The points of contact for Salt Lake City and Reno discussed the situation and agreed on the best interpretation given the overall objectives. They provided additional guidance to everyone collecting the data on how to interpret and record calls.

Another reason to monitor the data collection process is to maintain uniformity in procedures. If the instrument or procedures are found to be faulty after collection has begun and the team has to start over, costs in terms of time and resources can soar. An ounce of prevention can potentially be worth hundreds of employee hours and thousands of dollars.

After selecting partners, the NPR used a progression of collection techniques, starting with a list of questions about telephone service. Next, they conducted telephone interviews, and finally they visited partner sites. In the process, the NPR team corresponded with frontline employees, managers, union representatives, and others (National Performance Review, 1995, p. 3).

The Arlington, Texas, parks and recreation department developed a brief list of questions regarding front-desk customer service that it put to its benchmarking partners—for example: "Do you have a written document that gives a strategic overview of your company's approach to customer service? What types of customer service training do you provide for your employees? How many hours does it involve? Do you track retention rates? How do you measure customer satisfaction?" (Heller, 1994, p. 1). It then created a matrix to facilitate the comparison of all the data it had collected.

Conducting a Site Visit

Site visits are becoming more and more common among those seeking best practices, as well as among high-performing organizations that have been asked to be hosts. These visits help the team develop or further a sound partner relationship, as well as deepen the team's knowledge and understanding of its findings.

Since winning the Bertelsmann award in 1993, Phoenix has handled an untold number of inquiries and visits by curious institutions from both home and abroad. Vice President Gore's reinventing government team borrowed people from Phoenix and studied the city's deployment of computer and communication networks. And Arlington County, Virginia, which wanted to improve the level of service offered by its fire department, has conducted several site visits with Phoenix. Site visits also can link a number of partners and best practices. Charlotte first visited Seattle, then was subsequently asked by Arlington County to host a visit. Later, Seattle and Charlotte both were asked by Salt Lake City and Reno to host a visit.

Participants

The site visit team will be determined partially by the budget and schedule. Rarely can an organization afford to send everyone on the benchmarking team, and individuals' schedules do not always coordinate well with each other's or the hosting organization's. A general rule is to balance the strengths and weaknesses of the site visit team members, making sure their skills are complementary and do not dramatically overlap.

The project point of contact is in the best position to coordinate the site visit with his or her counterpart and should lead the site visit team. The visiting team should include one representative from major levels in the organization. For example, Reno's site visit team consisted of one technician, one analyst, and the project leader. The visiting team should also include experts in the pertinent processes—those who are articulate, skilled, qualified, and highly regarded—and, especially, experts in any technology that is perceived as vital to the process. When the information technology specialist from Salt Lake City experienced a scheduling conflict with the Seattle site visit, a knowledgeable substitute was found. Salt Lake City did not want to risk missing important information about Seattle's information technology.

The prestige, either real or perceived, attached to the members of the site visit team can elicit more favorable responses from the partner and a greater degree of cooperation. Having an elected or appointed official participate in the visit will add a further degree of importance to it, and the benchmarking organization can take advantage of the general willingness of others to oblige an elected representative or top administrator.

A goal is to cover all the bases within one to one and a half days using two or three people. More than two or three visitors can make the group unwieldy and somewhat unfocused. By selecting team members who can play multiple roles, you can keep the size of the team small. Obviously an agency that is benchmarking a large process or complicated practice may need more than three people on the site visit team.

Preparation and Logistics

Advance preparation is key to a successful site visit. Sending an unprepared task force just to "kick the tires" is not productive.

Before scheduling a site visit, the benchmarking team needs to develop a list of questions to help guide interviews during the visit and maintain uniformity among various partners. These site visit questions should cover process, staffing and logistics, information systems, obstacles to success, and managing the change, that is, making the transition to the new process. The questions should be sent to the partner before the actual visit so that the participants will have time to gather the required data and arrange for the appropriate people to be present and available.

Well before any site visits to Charlotte and Seattle, the benchmarking teams from Salt Lake City and Reno had developed a list of questions that they sent to officials in those cities. The list of questions did far more than probe the process under study; it asked for the history of the operation, the population served, the amount of political support for the process, what metrics the system collected, staffing needs, training procedures, hardware and software requirements, costs, and obstacles encountered (Keehley, 1995, pp. 13–17).

Another important aspect of preparation is to draw up, before the team departs, a detailed schedule of who will meet with whom and who will tour what facility when. When Charlotte and Seattle were benchmarked, officials there were sent formal agendas in advance of the actual visits (Keehley, 1995, p. 11). These agendas included the following information:

- Dates and times of arrivals, departures, and tours
- Discussion topics, such as overview, background, demographics, political influences, and process performance
- Questions developed by the site visit team
- Breaks and meals
- Names of individuals who would be present throughout the visit as well as at special meetings

Agendas typically go through several revisions. In conjunction with drawing up the schedule, appropriate team members should be assigned particular questions in conjunction with their meeting or touring assignments.

In addition to agendas, other materials may be provided. Charlotte and Seattle received in advance the internal data Salt Lake City and Reno had collected. This material gave them a sense of how Salt Lake City and Reno were currently performing.

In her role as project coordinator for Salt Lake City and Reno, the consultant prepared packets for the site visit teams as well as the hosts. The team package contained points of contact in the event that the consultant did not arrive, the visit agenda, the purpose of the visit, a list of participants, guidelines on how the visitors pledged to operate, and materials that the host sent in advance, such as organizational charts and background information. The packets sent to the hosts consisted of the visit agenda, the list of participants, the same set of guidelines, process maps from Salt Lake City and Reno, and the preliminary data collected.

Impact of the Visit on Partners

Guidelines help to minimize any negative impact on the day-to-day activities of the partners. The consultant for Salt Lake City and Reno specified that the teams had to arrive on time, not be interrupted from their work, respect the partner's time and space, and be very judicious in the questions they asked and the requests they made. The guidelines also promised that the visitors would stay on track, not become diverted, or divert their partners.

On-Site Etiquette

The time spent on the site visit should be reasonable and the visiting team small. The team should be prepared with information that can easily be obtained from public sources—for example, data on demographics or local economic conditions. The team may be divided into groups and paired with hosts so that they can collect a maximum of information from a variety of people in a short span of time. Team members should be prepared for a flurry of note taking and collecting of written documents, pictures, videos, and other materials. They should also be ready to gather the following essential information and items during the site visit:

- Names, model numbers, and manufacturer contact information for any equipment that seems essential to the best practice (for example, hardware and software)
- Instruction, training, or quality assurance manuals related to the process
- Information on performance indicators the host uses to monitor the process, and information on how they are collected and analyzed
- Job descriptions, skills, and qualifications of people who work within the process
- Process diagrams (the formal diagrams drawn up by production engineering) and supporting material

The comprehensive data-gathering tool developed by the Lynchburg, Virginia, fire department illustrates the scope of this undertaking. Officials there sought, in part, the following information from benchmarking partners (Public Management Group, "Fire and Emergency Medical Survey," n.d.):

1. Background: day and night county population; square mileage; contact person
2. Fire/EMS fiscal resources: personnel salaries; total appropriation; current budget
3. EMS service charges: who provides ambulance service; rate per mile
4. Department personnel allocation: administration; fire operations; inspections; arson investigators

5. Equipment resources: pumpers; ladders; rescue equipment; ambulances; hazardous material units
6. Racial composition of staff
7. Hazardous material management: response team; persons assigned per team; level of training; level of equipment; cross staffing from other teams
8. Public fire education: smoke detector information; education provided to different school levels; CPR and burn training
9. Code enforcement
10. Number of incidents
11. Deaths
12. Property loss

The visiting team should be aware of differences or gaps that might surface between partners. When Reno and Salt Lake City began to examine the customer referral process in Charlotte and Seattle, they noted certain differences in emphasis. In Seattle, where the process was organized by the mayor's office, customer complaints were received by a complaint investigator, who usually gave the problem high priority and resolved it quickly. In Charlotte, where the referral process was organized in the city manager's office, constituents' calls were received by a customer service representative, who then forwarded the issue to the appropriate department; follow-up varied and was often much slower. Team members needed to be aware of this difference, because in all probability it would become a factor in the importing process.

By the end of the site visit, team members should be able to sketch out at least a preliminary work flow diagram of the benchmarked process. They should understand all its components: inputs, the transformation through people, methods, materials, equipment, environment, and outputs.

Internal Partnerships and Visits
Up to this point, the discussion of site visits has applied only to external partners. Sharing best practices internally is another approach, one that private corporations have used for years. Now public services are coming to see the benefits of internal sharing of best practices. Revenue Canada's service improvement teams were the first to grasp that successful solutions should be shared

with each other—and shared immediately by electronic means. This realization led to the creation of the EXCELLENCE database of exemplary practices now being shared on electronic bulletin boards throughout Revenue Canada. The bulletin board may trigger more formal internal benchmarking studies.

Methods for "visiting" internal partners are deserving of attention. Internal partners may be located down the hall or down the stairs, but they should receive the same treatment as external benchmarking partnerships. Just because these departments inhabit the same building as the benchmarking unit does not mean they should be treated any less formally than external partners. A benchmarking team may have a tendency to adopt a more casual attitude and assume that internal partners have more availability than external partners. Such a misconception will lead to a less structured approach to data collection. Team members may subject internal partners to unscheduled drop-ins and redundant requests and questions. Haphazard data collection will lack uniformity, contain contradictions, annoy the host, and slow any project down.

For best results, all internal partnerships should be treated just like external ones: establish contacts, plan questions and agendas well in advance, alert partners to any changes, keep the visiting group small and the time spent on the partner's turf brief. In all likelihood, the benchmarking team will have to deal with an internal partner in the future, so our advice is to handle this relationship professionally and with discretion.

Postvisit Activities

Following the visit, the traveling team should brief other team members and process owners to acquaint them with the hard data as well as personal impressions. The visit does the benchmarker no good if what is discovered is not shared.

One team member should be assigned to collect and assimilate all the information gathered. This individual will be responsible for making backup copies, either hard or electronic, and storing the entire package in a safe but accessible location. If gaps are identified within the data, the point of contact can immediately call the benchmarking partner for additional data or clarification, if necessary.

Someone on the team should provide recognition and reward by thanking the partner's executives appropriately. "The quality of results of a best practice program is directly proportional to how receptive the target best practice companies are," writes one author (Doades, 1992, p. 16). Cooperation can be won by sharing something valuable in return for the partner's knowledge and time, such as a brief report summarizing what the team learned during the site visit. Such sharing will promote receptivity and a continuing dialogue.

Postvisit activities for the Salt Lake City–Reno project consisted of a one-day session with a dual purpose. In the first half of the meeting, team members reviewed what they had learned, determined what had really worked at each site, and identified differences that existed between the two sites. They spent the remaining time creating an implementation plan, a strategy for adaptation of the best practices by Salt Lake City and Reno.

The project consultant recognized that the two cities were now in the trickiest phase in the benchmarking process; from experience, she knew that benchmarking teams were likely to settle into inertia following the site visit. Chapter Nine addresses this critical period, when the benchmarking team's connection to its strategic goal is at its most tenuous.

Chapter Nine

Analyzing the Research and Selecting Best Practices to Adapt

So far, we have touched on three different areas of the benchmarking team's data collection:

1. Information about its own organization. This internal assessment helps the team establish a baseline for comparison with potential partners.
2. Preliminary data about potential partners. With selection criteria as a guide, this research helps the team to select the best match in terms of partnership.
3. Data from its actual partners. Gleaned from research, site visits, and partner surveys, these data enable the team to identify performance gaps and to isolate best practices.

The third category is the subject of this chapter. We begin by looking at exactly what this area of data analysis should accomplish when it is conducted properly.

Data Analysis

As soon as the site visit team has returned home, no doubt brimming over with information, data analysis begins. This is no time to take a break, because the team's knowledge and perceptions of the practices are fresh, and the team's eagerness to import them is at a peak. Waiting can dull the immediacy of these memories and the reasons for motivation. Exploit the returning team's optimism by having members tell other employees about what they discovered, either personally or in articles in the agency newsletter. They will transmit their enthusiasm for the project to the people who will be most affected by implementation.

From partner surveys or one or multiple site visits, the team no doubt has excavated a gold mine of new ideas and innovations. The temptation is either to throw up one's hands and say, "Where do I begin?" or to incorporate every bit of information into an implementation agenda. Clearly not all of these new ideas can be transformed into practical inputs, so the task now is to sift through the material to determine what is truly of value and what is just flashy facade. As with every other stage of a best practices effort, there are good methods and better methods, as well as potential pitfalls.

Data analysis should function as a good weed puller, helping the team to determine which practices are pertinent and feasible and which are beyond its reach in terms of resources and capabilities. Data analysis can also help the team identify strengths and opportunities, even outside the scope of the practice itself. Finally, data analysis allows a comparison of performance levels from different parts of the partner's process. Output should obviously be of the highest priority, but high output by inefficient means could be an indication of low quality. Efficiency and effectiveness measures should also be analyzed.

Data analysis is not without its pitfalls, and when a benchmarking team has invested much time, effort, and expense in the benchmarking project and is close to successful implementation, the last thing the team members want to experience is a loss of steam or misdirection, much less failure. Following the tips below will give some insurance against unwelcome outcomes at this point and will keep the team on track during the sometimes tedious task of review and analysis.

Avoid paralysis through overanalysis. The temptation to overanalyze all the data can bog down the team. Skilled facilitators, especially those with experience in quality management tools, can regularly reinforce the project objective and offer ways to help the group stay on task without being sidetracked by peripheral issues or other eye-catching material.

Be systematic. The Salt Lake City team compiled more information on practices than data or numbers. When the team members began to look at the research gathered through site visits, they spent about three hours brainstorming, discussing all the appealing practices they had observed in Charlotte and Seattle. With a list of forty practices in hand, the team evaluated each practice on two general dimensions: the importance of importing the practice to Salt Lake and whether the practice afforded quick or easy implementation. The most important recommendations were then prioritized. The top six recommendations on the final list were further developed and presented in greater detail to the Citywide Quality Steering Committee.

Be prepared for surprises. Keep an eye open for the unexpected—something of significance that the site visit team has overlooked perhaps, or a fluky piece of luck that could add an altogether new and promising dimension to the project. When the Salt Lake City team began evaluating the data it had collected, it was surprised to discover that its principal recommendation was only indirectly related to the practice being benchmarked. And after the Reno team determined how crucial new technology was going to be for improving the process, it was amazed to find that the software it had admired in Seattle and Charlotte had not been an expensive or complicated outside acquisition but had been developed by those cities in-house. Because Reno needed to select the new software and pilot the process within a short three months, this was a fortuitous discovery.

Understand similarities, but focus on differences. No doubt the practices uncovered will bear striking resemblance to one another. By looking only at similarities, though, there is a temptation simply to mimic the trends identified. Focusing on the differences and exceptions can lead to a more profound breakthrough, and a team that notes the areas where its organization's processes dramatically diverge from those of partners will find greater possibilities and opportunities for improvement and help ensure that their project remains distinctly their own.

Consider what happened when Salt Lake City and Reno benchmarked their processes with Charlotte and Seattle. At first glance the four teams appeared to have virtually the same processes, and the two benchmarking teams wondered what they could possibly learn from their partners. But once Salt Lake City and Reno began to scrutinize their processes, they identified some critical differences: divergences in the collection and management of data and important distinctions in overall mission and goals. In this case the difference literally made the difference.

Data Comparison

The more structure there is to the method of data comparison, the easier the task will be to manage. Allowing team members to plunge into the data on their own, without guidance, is counterproductive.

Before diving into the pool of data, set out the team's objectives: to discern the reasons for superior performance resulting from the best practice. This is a comparative analysis, with the agency's internal process used as the baseline. The analysis has two components: quantitative and qualitative comparisons. Some agencies, particularly those that rely on surveys for much of their research, prefer to hire a professional statistician to measure the quantitative results of their survey or designate an in-house department to do this. West Virginia's benchmarking team for the Employee Training project hired the University of Charleston's Robert C. Byrd Institute of Government Studies to put together a good partner questionnaire and then to provide the results in easy-to-understand graphs and charts. The qualitative assessment of these figures, however, remained in the hands of the benchmarking team itself, which determined what the figures meant in terms of best practice selection.

The evaluation should answer the following questions:

How innovative is the practice?

How cost-effective?

How will the practice affect the delivery of services?

How will it affect the performance gap?

Is there credible documentation that attests to customer satisfaction or success?

These questions should be in the back of everyone's mind throughout the process of data analysis. When the particulars of the research threaten to overwhelm the data analysis, refer back to these essential questions; they are the litmus test (National Center for Public Productivity, 1995). (You may want to refer back to Chapter One and its discussion of best practices to help you structure these questions.)

Dissection of the Process for Better Analysis

When nonquantifiable practices are the focal point, a different analytical approach may be necessary. Such practices work best when they are creatively adapted through abstraction. This is a conceptual process in which a model, rather than being copied whole, is dissected in order to assemble a better one. Importing, boiled down to its most basic elements, consists of these steps:

1. The benchmarking team observes an activity at a partner's organization.
2. From these observations, the team extracts the driving forces behind these practices, such as management style, empowerment, trust, communication style, and employee recognition and reward.
3. The team matches its own agency's practice on each driving force and determines to what degree those elements are currently employed or not employed.
4. The team identifies what will be required to make the practices work at its own agency: a change in procedures, a change in resources, a change in materials, a change in attitude, or a combination of all of the above.

By adding or strengthening desirable practices or eliminating less attractive ones, the benchmarking agency will build the chosen practice into its day-to-day operations. As it assesses its effort afterward, the agency will realize that, like a plastic surgeon, it has deconstructed what was there and reconstructed it to near perfection.

Council of Reviewers

Another way to proceed is to form a council of reviewers made up of project team members who did not participate in any of the site visits. Travel team members will recognize their host's material and tend to be biased in favor of it. The number of reviewers depends on how many partners and practices were examined—generally one or two more reviewers than the number of practices examined.

The Scoring Instrument

The reviewers can design a scoring mechanism containing questions relevant to their organization's priorities. When a uniform evaluation scheme is used, answers should indicate how well the practice meets expectations, fits parameters and constraints, and satisfies project objectives. The project coordinator may want to refer back to the original list of questions developed for the site visits. The instrument can use Likert scales (scales that apply a numbered rating system to questions), or reviewers can give open answers accompanied by actual grades in the form of percentages, with 100 percent being the maximum.

The Time Frame

"Walking barefoot through the data" aptly describes this stage of the project. The approach should be cautious, free from bias, and unhurried. The first goal of analysis and comparison is to get a broad view of what has been collected. Project coordinators may believe that their teams are well-oiled machines, but no team can be expected to churn through all the data in a matter of days and still be thorough. Allow whatever time is necessary for productive analysis—a few days at minimum and up to a few weeks for more complicated processes.

An off-site area for the critiquing session can avoid distractions and promote concentration. Find a comfortable room with all the necessary accoutrements: chalkboard, marker boards, flip charts, slide projector, and video and audio equipment. In a settled and relaxed environment, the team can examine the information gleaned from the partner surveys or from the notes, documents, reports, and diagrams that the visiting team has brought back from its site visit.

Quantitative Comparisons

The goal of the quantitative analysis is to locate and assess the opportunity for performance improvement within the benchmarking agency's current process. By taking the higher level of performance in the best practice and comparing it with the current level of performance in its own internal process, the team should be able to determine the degree of improvement that is possible. This opportunity or degree, better known as the performance gap, "provides an objective basis on which to act" (Camp, 1989b, p. 72). The dimensions of a performance gap can be negative, positive, or parity.

An assessment of a performance gap has three questions to answer: (1) How large is it? (2) Where is it? and (3) When does it occur? H. K. Vaziri (1992) writes: "Raw data are transformed into information that can be used to assess the current state of your organization and to target benchmarks. The findings must be evaluated in light of internal factors specific to each company" (p. 84), such as operating practices, production capabilities, and organizational structure, and external factors specific to the partner's industry, such as customer profile, market demographics, and technological development.

The first step in assessing performance gaps is to review the data as they come in and determine whether additional information is needed. When all the facts are in, the team selects the best performance for each factor as the benchmark and calculates the percentage difference between that level of performance and its own. Most often, the computation reveals a performance gap, but once in a while it may show a superiority (Vaziri, 1992, p. 85).

The performance gap analysis by West Virginia's Measuring Customer Satisfaction team examined the responses to a list of critical questions the team asked its thirteen partners. These questions were based on the team's own internal assessment and the research it had conducted concerning best practices. It assigned percentage values to these responses, and answers that showed a significant gap between baseline respondents and partners were identified. These questions served as the framework for the gap analysis. Once the gaps had been identified and quantified, the team qualitatively ascertained specific weaknesses in West Virginia's current processes. The inverse of these weaknesses could be said to be best practices, and we have identified them as such. Following is a summarized review of this team's findings:

Partner Survey Question One: What tools does your organization use to measure customer satisfaction?

Gap Analysis: All partners used questions and surveys; over 70 percent used telephone surveys, interviews, and customer focus groups as compared with 55.2 percent of the baseline respondents.

Areas of Weakness or Concern for West Virginia: State agencies use customer complaints as the dominant method for collecting information about customer satisfaction. State agencies do not as a whole employ enough measurement (data collection) tools.

Inferred Best Practice: Use of questions and surveys as the dominant method for collecting data regarding customer satisfaction.

Partner Survey Question Two: Do your organization's measurement tools make use of scales?

Gap Analysis: All of the partners but only 41.3 percent of the state agencies use scales in their measurement tools. In addition, 63.6 percent of the partners but only 27.6 percent of the baseline respondents use scales with values of one through five.

Areas of Weakness or Concern for West Virginia: 58.7 percent of state agencies do not use scales in measurement tools, and only 27.6 percent of the baseline respondents use a one-through-five scale.

Inferred Best Practice: Use of scales, particularly a one-through-five scale, as a tool for measurement.

Partner Survey Question Three: How does your organization validate surveys?

Gap Analysis: All partners use and validate surveys and employ professionals (survey research companies) to develop and validate their surveys. The majority of the state agencies (62.1 percent) do not use or validate surveys.

Areas of Weakness or Concern for West Virginia: 48.8 percent of state agencies do not use surveys; 61.1 percent of state agencies do not validate surveys; and only 17.2 percent of state agencies use a survey research company to develop and validate surveys.

Inferred Best Practice: Use and validation of surveys.

Partner Survey Questions Four and Five: If your organization uses customer focus, advisory, or user groups, how are members selected? What sampling technique does your organization use to collect data?

Gap Analysis: Almost none (only 3.4 percent) of the baseline respondents choose focus, advisory, or user group members in such a way that their opinions could be considered representative of the entire population; in contrast, the majority of the partners (66.7 percent) use probability sampling techniques. Almost none of the partners use nonprobability sampling as their sole means of collecting data, whereas 44.8 percent of the baseline respondents do.

Areas of Weakness or Concern for West Virginia: Of the state agencies that use customer focus, advisory, or user groups, a very low percentage of them use a nonbiased method of selecting participants. The overreliance on the nonprobability sampling technique by state agencies ensures biased data.

Inferred Best Practice: Use of sampling principles when possible to guarantee the accuracy of data.

Partner Survey Question Six: How often does your organization sample or collect data to measure customer satisfaction?

Gap Analysis: The vast majority of partners collect data on a cyclic basis, whereas the majority of the baseline agencies do not.

Areas of Weakness or Concern for West Virginia: As compared with the partners, the state as a whole is not continually collecting data to measure customer satisfaction. Partners are measuring continually and also find value in collecting data at intervals, that is, semiannually and biannually.

Inferred Best Practice: Continual data measurement plus data collection at intervals—that is, semiannually and biannually.

Partner Survey Question Seven: Who analyzes the customer satisfaction data for your organization?

Gap Analysis: The vast majority of the partners (81.8 percent) hire a consulting firm to analyze their data, but only 10.3 percent of the baseline agencies do so.

Areas of Weakness or Concern for West Virginia: The state generally does not use statisticians to perform analysis, there are only a few formally trained personnel within state organizations to analyze the data, and very few agencies use external consulting firms to analyze the collected data.

Inferred Best Practice: Use of an outside consulting firm (statistician) to analyze data.

Partner Survey Question Eight: What type of analysis is performed on the collected data?

Gap Analysis: From the partners' response, it appears that a combination of descriptive and inferential statistics is necessary to provide managers with the information they need to improve customer satisfaction. Of the partners, 63.6 percent used both inferential and descriptive statistical analysis; only 6.9 percent of the baseline respondents used both.

Areas of Weakness or Concern for West Virginia: Exclusive use of descriptive statistics by state agencies is very high. A very low percentage of state agencies use both descriptive and inferential analysis.

Inferred Best Practice: Inferential and descriptive analyses because descriptive analysis alone is inadequate.

Partner Survey Question Nine: If contacts that compose the customer's interaction with your organization are identified, does your organization weight (prioritize) the relative importance of these contacts?

Gap Analysis: Only 9.1 percent of the partners do not identify customer contacts. In contrast, 75.9 percent of the baseline respondents do not identify the customer contacts.

Areas of Weakness or Concern for West Virginia: Most of the state customer satisfaction measurement systems do not gather information about the customer's interaction with the agencies, precluding the study of customer satisfiers and dissatisfiers and the identification of actions that will lead to increased satisfaction.

Inferred Best Practice: Identification of customer contacts as an important means of rating an organization's performance.

Partner Survey Question Ten: Does the data analysis allow your organization to identify critical events that result in customer satisfaction or dissatisfaction?

Gap Analysis: Of the partners, 90.9 percent indicate that their system allows them to identify critical events, as compared with 69 percent of the baseline agencies. The partners' response to this question was consistent with their response to question nine, but the baseline was not consistent. The two items are contingent on one another. One cannot have an understanding of critical events without first knowing all the contacts.

Areas of Weakness or Concern for West Virginia: To a large degree the state's data analysis of the customer satisfaction measurement system does not allow the state to identify critical events that result in customer satisfaction or dissatisfaction.

Inferred Best Practice: Data analysis to identify critical events that result in customer satisfaction or dissatisfaction.

Qualitative Comparisons

This more descriptive analysis revolves around the qualitative components of the benchmarking partner's procedures and methods and can be drawn from the quantitative report. Now that the team has identified and quantified performance gaps, it turns to what these gaps say. The qualitative analysis should answer two key questions: (1) What does the benchmark partner do that is the same as we do? (2) What does the partner do that is different?

A public agency cannot expect to choose among several excellent practices that it qualifies as best practices without setting standards by which to judge the practices first. On the surface, the practices may seem equally exceptional, but just because they work wonders for public agency A or corporation B does not mean they will work as well for another entity. For each practice under consideration, the team should address certain selection criteria. We describe some of these criteria in Chapter One; benchmarking teams can use them as a starting point, adding or subtracting items in accordance with their own needs. Additionally, the team may wish to answer the following questions before moving ahead to implementation:

Issues and Needs Addressed

What issues and needs does the practice address?

Are there any additional outcomes from the practice?

Effect and Benefit of Adopting the Practice

What level of satisfaction with the practice exists within each stratum of the partner's organization?

How well has the practice responded to the needs of clients?

Has the practice produced any unforeseen benefits for management, staff, or clients?

Cost-Benefit Ratio

What are the costs that pertain directly to the practice?

Is the practice actually cost-effective?

Will your organization incur any unanticipated start-up costs? If so, how long will it take to pay these expenses off?

Do the benefits outweigh the costs, or do the costs outweigh the benefits? Does the practice produce savings, circumvent cost, or generate income?

Service Delivery

In what way does the practice enhance service delivery? Are more clients served? Is response or waiting time reduced? Is there a lessening of paperwork?

Will the new process temporarily disrupt customer interaction and service but ultimately improve it?

Will it confuse your customers?

Have customers been alerted to the forthcoming changes?

Will it slow down response time?

How long do you estimate customers will need to adjust to the new way of doing things?

Longevity

How do you rate the practice's potential for long-term survival and performance?

Does the practice have measurable, sustained results?

Chances of Success in the Organization's Environment

How much upheaval does the practice involve?

Will the changes be accepted in the current environment? Will they incite rebellion?

What preventive measures can be taken to deter any anticipated rebellion?

Is your organization a loose confederation of autonomous individuals suddenly facing a new practice that depends on teamwork or on assembly-line-like process?

Degree to Which Each Practice Will Close the Performance Gap

Will the practice under consideration bring you 50 percent closer to the top performance level? 75 percent? 99 percent? Or will it put you 10 percent over the top?

Is your goal simply reliable, guaranteed improvement, or will your agency settle for nothing but the best?

Obstacles to Success

What currently existing obstacles will impede the successful implementation of this practice?

How can these obstacles be neutralized?

Are the requirements for importing beyond your organization's means? Do they exceed your buying power? Take too much time? Is your staff too limited? Is the practice too complex for the limited capabilities and skills of the current process owners?

Is the degree of workability of this practice high or low?

Is the practice cost-effective and easy to implement?

Transferability

Will the practice be easily replicated?

Is it worthy of adoption, or is its appeal limited?

Will the practice require a change in management style or a new service concept?

Is it a reasonably stable process?

Is the practice related to unique aspects of the partner or to a key leader or manager?

Technology

Has someone from within your management systems department assessed the need for technology?

Is this process technology innovative?

Does your organization have the requisite technology in place?

Will this new technology require extensive training?

Presenting Results to Management

Will the results be easy to follow?

Are they in accordance with the reigning management philosophy?

Will the best practice require legislative or statutory reform?

Overall Rating

Based on the answers to the previous questions, what are the practice's key strengths and weaknesses?

After identifying what areas needed improvement through gap analysis, the West Virginia team drew up a number of recommendations to present to the governor:

> *Recommendation I:* All divisions and agencies within the State of West Virginia should have a well-defined and well-articulated Customer Satisfaction Measurement System.
>
> *Recommendation II:* There should be a central point of leadership for mentoring and overseeing the Customer Satisfaction Measurement Systems within the State of West Virginia, and there should be a cardinal body that oversees the measurement system.
>
> *Recommendation III:* State agencies should seek the expert assistance of professionals in developing and maintaining their customer satisfaction measurements. This can be done through the following two options:
> 1. The most effective and efficient option is to have an external consulting firm.
> 2. For agencies that are unable to accommodate external consulting firms, a core group of statisticians within State government should be used to develop and maintain a Customer Satisfaction Measurement System [West Virginia Benchmarking Project, 1996, Ch. 4, p. 1].

These recommendations were general and did not focus on some of the more specific items addressed in the gap analysis. At the conclusion of this report, however, the team included a list of suggestions, or critical success factors, that it deemed essential for implementation.

Communication of Findings

Before developing strategies to address and eliminate performance gaps, the team should share its findings with those who have had input in the process and with those who will be affected by the changes. Sharing with the process owners improves commitment to the plan and understanding of the expected levels of improvement. Furthermore, ongoing communication with the partner minimizes the chances of misinterpretation and increases the value of feedback. Frequent updates on methodology, key findings, and recommendations should be made to management, suppliers, customers, and other employees.

By describing the practice in language that conveys what the practice will look like in its own agency rather than in the partner's language, the benchmarking team puts its own agency's distinctive stamp on the practice, making it more familiar to the process owners and thereby strengthening the buy-in process.

Presentation of Recommendations

The climax of a benchmarking project is the team's presentation to management or the oversight committee. This test has only two outcomes: pass or fail. Similar to a doctoral candidate's defense of his or her dissertation or proposal, the project coordinator and presentation team will be defending their recommendations, as well as the time, effort, and dollars they have expended in pursuit of the best practices. In this meeting, the team presents its findings, its recommendations, and evidence supporting its conclusions. Nothing can do more damage to the cause than a poor presentation, so we present some guidelines to help the presenter:

Anticipate questions or possible drawbacks to the findings. Think about your audience and imagine their reaction. If a department head is present, she may be very interested in implementation issues. On the other hand, an elected official may ask more questions about the budget or the impact on customers.

Assume that the people to whom you are making your presentation are benchmarking novices. Some of the data you collected during your project may have been complex. Your job is to present this information with clarity and simplicity.

Aim for the quickest and largest impact by using bold yet simple diagrams, charts, and graphs. The presentation may be accompanied by a written report or immediately followed by a report so as not to draw attention from the presentation. West Virginia's Measuring Customer Satisfaction team communicated its findings in a written report to the governor, elucidating significant discrepancies between partners and baseline respondents through pie charts and bar graphs. Concise and easy to read, this report got to the crux of the issues quickly and in a way that was never burdensome or confusing to the reader.

Indicate clearly the estimated costs of implementing changes and the expected outcomes and benefits. Also prepare a formal budget and time line for introducing the changes.

Prepare with a dress rehearsal. Preparation for the presentation can be intense and stressful. To judge the effectiveness of your performance, gather a group of nonparticipating staff members or clients and give a dress rehearsal. Have the members of the audience simulate a question-and-answer session immediately following the presentation and complete a rating questionnaire. The topics of their questions and their ratings are a good indication of the strengths and weaknesses of your argument. Use their feedback to refine or reorganize your material.

Prepare a rough action plan in a table format. By summarizing the presentation material, the table makes it more easily understood by management as well as employees and staff members who will be affected by the changes. The prospective action plan will also serve as a tool to allay the doubt and disbelief of individuals who reacted to the gap analysis.

Now that the data brought back by the site visit teams have been analyzed, performance gaps assessed, practices reviewed and rated, and recommendations accepted, the time is at hand for benchmarking's penultimate stage: adapting the practice to home.

Chapter Ten

Adapting and Implementing Best Practices

Once best practices have been identified and selected and the team's recommendations have been accepted by management, the focus of the project now turns to incorporating these best practices into the organization, transforming it from being a business-as-usual organization to a superachiever. Like every other step in the benchmarking process, implementing a best practice requires a good plan.

Understanding an Action Plan

The action plan is tied directly to the organization's mission and vision. It is the framework for introducing change, the detailed road map for the agency's journey toward its improvement goals.

Most important to Salt Lake City and Reno's success at adapting their newly found best practices was their development of a detailed action (or implementation) plan that carefully considered the following questions and issues:

- What is the ideal way to do business?
- What is the ideal process?
- Where, within the city, does the ideal process cross departments and branches?
- Where should the new process be piloted or tested?

The benchmarking team's recommendations became a charter to the implementation team, which used it to develop blueprints for introducing change, just as federal laws and regulations bring to life the provisions of the Constitution. The function of the implementation team is to "translate the benchmark findings into statements of how their organization will change" (Camp, 1989a, p. 175). The team must determine the stages the organization will pass through as it evolves over time and ultimately how the organization will look when it arrives at the finish line—what Camp (1989a) calls the "achievable endpoint" (p. 179).

The action plan takes a multifaceted and complicated implementation process and presents it in a format people can grasp: as a whole concept and in the form of tangible tasks. Well-prepared action plans provide the who, what, why, when, where, and how of implementing change. They fulfill these practical considerations by addressing the following issues:

- The relationship between agency objectives and proposed changes. To which objectives and goals do the changes relate? Has the plan made this relationship explicit?
- Tasks that need to be accomplished according to priority.
- Responsible parties for the overall project and specific tasks, with one individual personally responsible for the completion of each task.
- Deadlines for tasks that are realistic but challenging.
- Resources needed to accomplish change, such as funds, personnel hours, or special equipment.

When Reno considered these issues, it decided to begin the implementation process in the City Manager's Office and the Community Development Office. Reno administrators hoped that successful implementation in those two areas would encourage other departments to join. The team believed that by allowing departments to volunteer, they would secure long-term gains that would outweigh any short-term achievements stemming from a mandate that all departments participate from the beginning.

Salt Lake City adopted a similar strategy in that other municipal departments were not forced to participate. Rather, the Department of Public Services took the lead. Building on the benchmarking team's original vision of "one call for all services" and the insights gained from the site visit, the implementation team first revisited the in-house systems and processes with eyes open to new possibilities. The team then reported to the citywide Quality Steering Committee with a list of recommendations.

Developing an Action Plan

A detailed implementation plan is developed after the practices for importing have been accepted. A broad action plan prepared for the presentation of recommendations can serve as the guide in devising a more specific and exhaustive plan.

Task planning is the "preparation of a detailed description of activities to be implemented to accomplish desired changes," so it is important that the selected best practices can be translated into specific, implementable recommendations (Bruder and Gray, 1994, pp. S13, S16). William Gay of the Public Innovation Group (1992) suggests that the plan be a written document for managers to use in monitoring progress, always in the form of a working draft. According to Gay, action planning consists of two activities: planning tasks and developing stakeholder commitment to those activities.

An action plan uses standard project management procedures, answering the basic question: Who will do what by when? It considers major tasks, time lines, milestones, pilot activities, and end points. A number of software database programs are available for monitoring projects. Exhibit 10.1 shows Reno's action plan for its importing process.

Choosing an Approach to Implementation

Bruder and Gray (1994) have identified approaches that implementation teams often adopt. The first is the "try harder" approach (p. S13), which seeks limited improvement based on acknowledged discrepancies between the benchmarking organization's performance and that of the partner. Obviously this approach does the entire benchmarking project a disservice. What the organization needs now is fundamental change—perhaps not a complete overhaul but certainly exhaustive revisions in current strategies and processes. To focus on short-term, immediate improvements defeats the whole purpose of benchmarking.

In the 1970s the NYCTA system was rapidly approaching a serious state of disrepair. Generous capital funding in the early 1980s allowed NYCTA to get good results by throwing money at the processes that needed fixing, but certain problems remained, such as swelling inventory and rising storage and operating costs. As the money dried up, NYCTA looked at how it could improve inventory management, and through a largely internal assessment, it was able to make small improvements. It was clearly "trying harder," making an honest stab at improvement and with moderate success. When NYCTA decided to conduct a benchmarking analysis of world-class organizations, pervasive, measurable progress occurred. It used best practices from both the private and public sectors, with some remarkable results in rising standards of service performance and inventory efficiency. In the process, employee morale improved radically because both employees and managers were involved throughout the benchmarking project and were accountable for the results. Had NYCTA settled for limited, short-term improvements, it would have probably found itself back at square one: in disrepair, with no funds, and without the strong support of staff (Bruder and Gray, 1994).

The second approach to implementation that Bruder and Gray outlined is the "emulate the best-in-class" (p. S13) response. This amounts to copycatting, which does little more than maintain the status quo—but not for long, because while other organizations are furthering their progress, the benchmarking agency is playing catch-up.

The implementation team's attitude toward implementation should be aggressive and positive, and it should seek to err on the side of overzealousness: "Leapfrog the competition," advise Bruder and Gray (p. S13). A good practice is to combine research from a number of best-practice organizations, picking and choosing what appears to hold the best possibilities for success. In West Virginia's One-Stop Business Registration project, members of the project team realized early on that they were pioneers in a virtual wilderness. There were no existing practices to adapt. They had to combine knowledge from different partners for the state to become best-in-class itself, setting a precedent in terms of service and technology.

The questions that follow provide a general framework for the team as it begins the challenge of importing a best practice to its own agency:

Exhibit 10.1. Reno Action Plan.

Action Step	October 1–15	October 15–31	November 1–15	November 15–30	December 1–15	December 15–31	January 1–15	January 15–31
Decide on System								
Meet with management committee	●							
Talk with data processing	●							
Brief original benchmarking team	●							
Get department information (system interface, point of contact)	●							
Establish selection committee	●							
Obtain purchasing requirements		●						
Make selection		●						
Determine other hardware or software requirements		●						
Purchase System								
Take to council			●					
Finalize purchase of system				●				
Finalize purchase(s) of other hardware/software			●	●				
Notify supplier(s)				●				

Installation

Provide detail requirements to vendor

Coordinate with department(s)
on installation

Install other hardware or software
if required

Install new system

Train systems people

Implementation

Create reference manuals

Begin using system

Train end users; provide manual

Support end users

1. Did the team establish a reasonable time frame for interim steps?
2. Will the organization commit resources of money and team member time to the project?
3. Has the team included customers? If so, at what stages?
4. Has the team built in test points and opportunities to modify the direction?
5. What measures will be used to prove success? These measures must be installed in advance to establish a baseline or allow for comparisons with previous practices.

As Bruder and Gray (1994) rightly suggest, there are times when change cannot be implemented properly until the rules are changed. Sometimes an agency's entire operating procedure needs modification. In other cases, laws need to be changed before the team can implement improvements. Anticipating these potential monkey wrenches can help ensure that certain performance gaps are closed—and stay closed.

Instituting a Pilot Project

Before implementation actually begins, the team should test the proposed solutions in a real-life situation. That step reduces the chance of making fundamental changes before they are proved effective, and it allows for adjustments. In the same way, implementers should make the necessary changes to process components on a trial basis. Performance data are collected throughout the pilot project, according to a measurement plan developed earlier. If the data show that performance is meeting expectations, then changes can be formalized and solidified within the organization. If the data fall short of anticipated levels, another attempt can be made at refitting the changes.

One important benefit of a pilot project is that persons who will be affected by a change have the chance to test it or observe others testing it. This step is a hands-on experimentation period, and process owners can offer suggestions on how to tweak the changes to squeeze even more effectiveness out of them. The opportunity to contribute to the project will impart to personnel a sense of ownership and increase their future acceptance of the changes.

Forming the Implementation Team

Implementation teams play a critical role in success. The number of teams will depend on the complexity and magnitude of change. In the case of Reno, one team was formed to coordinate the activities of divisions and offices, and another team spearheaded software selection. The teams shared some members, which helped assure continuity and achievement of goals. After deciding the number of teams that are necessary, the project coordinator or consultant must determine the team's makeup. Who joins, who does not, and what is the rationale for each decision? In most cases, the implementation team members will be the same as the former benchmarking team members, especially if the benchmarking team was carefully selected. Why establish a new team or series of teams to implement the practice when the benchmarking team has been steeped in the research data for months? Sometimes the recommendations specify who should be on the implementation team. In Reno, the implementation team expanded to include people who had been involved in earlier stages of the benchmarking project.

Additionally, Bruder and Gray (1994) advise, "Whatever function you are benchmarking, it always is critical that you involve a variety of individuals from that function in the benchmarking analysis" (p. S13). West Virginia's One-Stop Business Registration team included among its list of recommendations the suggestion that the governor appoint an implementation team composed of middle management personnel from the affected agencies; it also recommended that the One-Stop benchmark team be represented on the implementation team for purposes of continuity.

Including one member each from the categories of first-line supervisor, technician, and administrative staff can improve the chances of successful implementation. Because the team will be asking others to change their daily operations, a team composed of managers only may have less influence with frontline workers than a team that includes members who are in a similar position as, or who have worked previously with, the frontline workers. Fewer employees will question the implementation activities if more people have been involved in determining the approach.

The champion smooths the way for the team's work by acting as a goodwill ambassador to other individuals the team will encounter, and he or she mediates any disputes that arise. An implementation team that must constantly defend its actions will never complete the implementation. Instead it will exhaust time, energy, and resources in countering objections. Having a champion will permit the team to focus on its mission of bringing the best practice to fruition within the organization.

Implementation teams, like any other group with a shared objective, require a leader or facilitator to assist with decisions and coordinate individual actions within the implementation plan. This person should also report to the champion any stumbling blocks or adversity the team encounters. The team leader functions both as a cohesive force within the group and as the point of information exchange between group members who may not have direct access to each other.

Depending on the number of elements of the practice and the number of individuals contained within the process, the team leader may want to create several small implementation teams instead of one. For instance, if within the practice there is an element of management style, the coordinator can bring together a team nucleus of process owners (managers) supported by a few employees on whom the new management technique will impinge.

Whether the implementation team is new or a carryover from the benchmarking team, the latter must finish its work by providing detailed recommendations on the changes to be made, accompanied by all background material. Once the implementation crew has been brought together, the benchmarking team explains the project to them. After training has been completed and the project handed off to the implementation team, members of the benchmarking team should be available for consultation. If implementation team members need to visit the benchmark partner to observe the best practice in action, the benchmarking team can arrange this short visit for observation.

Recruiting Ancillary Team Members: Customers and Suppliers

Customers and suppliers may be peripheral to the department and process, but that does not mean they cannot or should not play a part in implementation. If any aspect of their daily operations will change due to the new practice, customers and suppliers should at the very least receive advance notice of the pending changes.

A method that ensures more inclusive participation is to seek customer and supplier opinions and suggestions once the practice has been chosen. The importation of new practices may require customers and suppliers to change their familiar and possibly long-established procedures. It may mean new contacts, new telephone numbers, or new ways of communication for the suppliers to learn. Customers and suppliers who are encouraged and coached to play an active role in implementation may be able to assist in unanticipated ways. For instance, Charlotte initiated its continuous improvement effort by conducting focus groups with constituents and discovered that constituents had difficulty determining when they should call the county for a particular service and when they should call the city. As a result of this input, Charlotte decided to install a more centralized customer service center.

Importing Success

Importing is only as successful as the planning behind it. Determining the best possible location and timing is integral to implementation, and anticipating objections and pretesting strategies are indispensable precautions in an often delicate process. We have identified several key factors in successful implementation.

Involve Others

In Reno, as elsewhere, involving others was one of the most critical aspects of adapting the practice. Given the nature of the new process, it was apparent that many other people should be involved to ensure success. For instance, the benchmarking team's vision for the customer referral process was that constituents could call any department, request any information, and essentially get what they needed. To accomplish this, every department had to have access to the system for use as a reference tool for communicating with others about work requirements. Therefore all departments ultimately had to be involved. Yet the team and the city manager did not want to mandate that departments migrate to the new process and system, an approach that tends to have a negative effect on staff. Instead they first informed the department heads about the changes and then asked for departmental representatives to help define system requirements and provide input along the way. This approach enticed others to participate without dictating that they do so.

Be Adaptable

Good data analysis allows the benchmarkers to look beyond the immediate scope of the project. For example, the most important recommendation that Salt Lake City made was only tangentially related to its customer referral process. The team had been impressed with the way its partners, Charlotte and Seattle, used public information officers (PIOs) in each of their departments. The PIOs interacted with the community and with each other in a way that created an image of a responsive, concerned government working to inform and serve its constituents. They took the initiative to prevent or minimize problems rather than have problems surface over the telephone or in the press, and they communicated regularly with the customer service center to be sure callers were given the most up-to-date information and that the center staff was prepared to deal with any unexpected surge in calls.

Having observed this role of the PIOs, Salt Lake City constructed a similar scenario within its own administrative ranks. The departmental PIOs would be led by the mayor's PIO, they would be linked to service districts that had already been established informally, and they would integrate community outreach and council issues. This use of PIOs in Salt Lake City is an excellent example of the synergy one hopes to see result from the site visit. The team felt so strongly that the PIO was an integral part of Charlotte's and Seattle's success that they risked going outside their immediate charter to make this item their top recommendation.

Expect Both Incremental and Wholesale Change

Some aspects of the imported practice will be incremental in nature; others may represent more wholesale kinds of change. For example, Reno and Salt Lake City began implementation of a similar process but from different starting points. Each city reached out to constituents and citizens in its surrounding county to tell them how to get the most from the new city information services. In the past Reno had used very little automation in its customer referral process, so its immediate task was to decide to install a new automated system to correspond to its newly designed process. Salt Lake City approached the process a little less dramatically. Because it already had an automated system in place, with regular reports generated by utilities and through the mayor's office, its first step was to pilot modifications in the Public Services Department, campaigning within the city to encourage its use.

Indoctrinate the Users

Sometimes implementation is hampered because of existing regulations or legislative impediments. In order to make the new process standard operating procedure, the implementation team needs to record details of the process in operations manuals, thereby recording the new process for posterity. And once the process owners have observed or experimented with the changes, the implementation team will need to cement the new procedures in the minds of all who may come into contact with those procedures by holding training sessions for management, vendors, and constituents alike. One of the Reno team's greatest concerns was that the process owners receive manuals as reference tools, along with training on how to use the manuals. This two-pronged provision for manuals and training became an important vendor selection criterion.

A secondary means of formal inculcation is adapting the data collection methods used throughout the benchmarking project into the performance measurement system normally used within the department. These performance measures established for internal and partner performance comparison can become part of the regularly scheduled reporting system.

Understand the Human Element

Importing a best practice requires more than just organizational or technological readjustments. It is far more difficult to motivate people to change their attitudes and methods than it is to install new software or design a survey form. R. C. Camp (1989a) advises giving behavior "equal attention as task considerations. Gaining acceptance, concurrence, and commitment is vital to the success of your new practice" (p. 191). Benchmark findings can often be traumatic, particularly to those who are new to the process or accustomed to different management styles. It can be safely said that if the organization does not have a cooperative employee base, the benchmarking project will probably fail. Overcoming fear and resistance can be met by combining four strategies:

1.   *Disseminate information.* Appoint an individual within each department who can be a resident benchmarking expert. This person should be supportive of the benchmarking effort and sufficiently well informed to field employees' questions or concerns. Agency or department newsletters are also a useful way to share information and allay anxieties.

2.   *Provide training.* Implementation is not a time to test personnel on their ability to adapt quickly. Provide training to introduce employees to the practice and to persuade them that the practice will bring significant rewards and benefits to all parts of the organization, either directly or indirectly. Picture the trainer as an attorney arguing a case before a jury. The attorney's objective is to elicit a favorable decision from the jury in regard to her argument. Similarly the trainer ultimately seeks employee approval of the new practice.

3.   *Allow for nonthreatening experimentation with the new process.* Museums today entertain the public with hands-on exhibits and other "it's-fun-to-find-out" approaches. Similarly allow the process owners and those whom the new practice will affect to work with it or in it, to adjust to it, and to dabble in the new medium like experimenting artists. Within the experimentation period, personnel should be free of constraints, expectations, specific assignments, and deadlines.

4.   *Establish a new reward and compensation structure based on new performance measures.* Avoiding the stick when instituting changes does not call for avoiding the carrot as well. To assist in the uptake of the new practice, construct an incentive program around the new performance measures.

Produce Tangible Products

The fire chief of Arlington County, Virginia, Ed Plaugher, realized that if his department was to be successful at its initial best practices effort, it had to produce some real, discernible products that the citizens could see, feel, hear, and react to. Otherwise, he said, "people are just going to say that [benchmarking] was just another exercise" (Plaugher, 1995). Without a doubt, people need to see tangible goods to support this kind of effort. Chief Plaugher also noted that this phenomenon is hardly limited to citizens; it is true for internal customers as well—in his case, the "firefighters who do the serving," in addition to the succeeding layers of management, reaching all the way up to the county manager. "Our people are very pragmatic and very straightforward," the chief adds, describing their orientation as "Show me why we are doing this." "Every day," he continues, "firefighters in Arlington County put water on fires. They can personally witness that if they do that, and do it properly, the fire goes out. [So they wonder], 'Why should we be making all this other stuff? What does this have to do with my job?'" The chief believes strongly that public administrators must be able to tie those two thought processes together in order to have a successful benchmarking project.

Use Public Relations Positively

A successful benchmarking project is an ideal way to promote the continued use of benchmarking. The organization can publicize its success internally through organizational newsletters and externally through press conferences and newspapers; forward significant results to industry journals such as *Governing, PA Times, Public Management,* and *Quality Progress;* and submit success stories to the Alliance for Redesigning Government to include in the Web site database. The more positive publicity that is generated, the greater the support will be from the administration and the public for benchmarking efforts.

Measuring Performance

Throughout the implementation process, it is a good idea to confirm the validity and worth of the solutions. "Compare progress against pre-defined milestones, determining the causes of variances, " advises Camp (1989a, pp. 205–206). If the outcomes do not meet with preset standards, modifications may be in order. On the other hand, do not expect the full force of the change to emerge within one day. Establish a trial period, with the length depending on the size and intricacy of the changes being made. If a subdivision of an organization is changing five or six steps of a process, it may choose to allow two weeks before measuring performance. The same amount of time may not suffice for a fifty-point tune-up of a function involving an entire organization.

Modifying As You Go

Implementation is a fluid, open-ended process. Be willing to consider other changes that might be required and the potential for maximizing return on resources invested in improvement. You may discover that your organization needs a second or even a third trial. Also, the implementation team should allow for further adjustments to be made based on the suggestions of the process owners that arise during the initial trial period.

Importing a Best Practice: A Long-Term Process

Ideas that work in one locality may fail in another if there is improper cultivation. An agency may appear to be addressing a social problem or seeking improvement when in actuality it has not analyzed its internal processes or the characteristics of the municipality from which the program is being borrowed. Paul Epstein, formerly of the New York City Mayor's Office, has labeled this phenomenon "pilot programmitis" (Barrett and Greene, 1993, p. 37).

Stakeholders covet solutions that have the strength and effectiveness of best practices but can have a hard time comprehending and accepting the extended efforts and long-term commitment required by a benchmarking initiative. In the public sector, innovation gets noticed because of its scale. For example, when the IRS Cincinnati service center began accepting electronically transmitted tax returns, the public and press were captivated. The practice was innovative and set a new internal standard for all IRS processing centers. The initial program, however, was limited to the 1040EZ, the form used by taxpayers with simple returns. Over time public attention declined dramatically, even though many other types of tax returns were added to the list and other IRS centers began to implement the practice. It took several years for the IRS to implement these new practices fully; it remained committed in spite of waning public interest. Successful benchmarking is like a sine wave. The publicity ebbs and flows, but you must be vigilant about implementing over the long run.

The major disadvantage of importing a best practice is that the multistage evaluation and introspection demanded by benchmarking do not attract the media attention or the public support that the organization might like (Barrett and Green, 1993, p. 37). Public agencies that are being pressured to justify how their dollars are being spent may feel a need to expedite the benchmarking process, but the ways they choose might be counterproductive.

Benchmarking is both expansive and introspective in nature. It takes time, it is ongoing, and it reaches into the nooks and crannies of the organization.

Recognizing Possible Pitfalls

Successful implementation may be assured by avoiding pitfalls. Be wary of recognized land mines discovered by others.

Shortcuts

Knowing what attracts good press, many public officials have tried to imitate an entire program that has proved itself successful in another venue, incorrectly assuming that exact mimicry of a best practice will get them the desired results more quickly. The purpose of undertaking a best practice search, however, is not to exactly replicate the practice that worked for another. This copycat approach occasionally does work, but the randomness of its success could put a project at risk. Copycatting is indicative of a lack of understanding of the power and potential of benchmarking and best practices. It often results from industrial tourism and superficial internal examinations and external research.

Tearing down an old process just to install an entirely new one based on mimicry wastes valuable time and money, destroys morale, and practically guarantees failure at achieving the organization's goals. It resembles industrial tourism in that it focuses on the cheap thrills without any self-analysis. The outcome from a copycat process can actually lower performance, inflating the performance gap instead of shrinking it. Without understanding the philosophies, practices, and processes employed by model agencies, cloning their methods and procedures could be a disaster.

Suppose that state officials in charge of roads in Alaska decided to benchmark with other states. They would be wise to consider the factors that make them unique. For example, permafrost, the permanently frozen subsoil that is common in Alaska, is not found in the lower forty-eight states. Mimicking the road depth dug by crews in other states would seriously jeopardize the success of Alaska's improvement efforts.

Unlike other methodologies for improvement, best practices require maximum commitment and wholehearted effort. Although the search for best practices may demand more from an organization, it produces greater results in return.

Lack of Cooperation

Another importing pitfall is a lack of cooperation within the locality itself—between city hall and the city council, between businesses and government, or between agencies (Barrett and Greene, 1993, p. 37). This was certainly the case in West Virginia's One-Stop Business Registration project, where agencies were resistant to relinquishing their turf. The only way around this major roadblock was for the benchmarking team to recommend to the governor specific legislative reforms to make the process change mandatory.

When the success of a process hinges on the cooperation of two or more public entities, importing a new procedure requires the agreement of both parties to go along with the changes that will soon be delivered by the benchmarking unit. Many departments and agencies compete with one another for funds, creating a barrier to the cooperation needed for successful benchmarking. Long before importing gets under way, the benchmarking champion should begin to change the spirit of the relationship from one of competition to one of cooperation. In West Virginia's One-Stop Business Registration project, the benchmarking team was composed of a representative from each of the five agencies that would be affected by the new process, thus helping to ensure that no one agency was prioritized over another and that ownership of the process remained strong.

Exporting Success

The more an agency exports the new process or improvement to other parts of the organization, the better the return is on its benchmarking investment. A champion who regularly encourages widespread implementation of a best practice will add strength to a good implementation plan. Charlotte's champion had a strong philosophy about exporting her success to other parts of the city. Her strategy was to demonstrate the benefits of her new service clearly to resistant departments within the city and regularly lobby them to use it. When Salt Lake City piloted its new process in the Public Services Department, it intended the Mayor's Office to follow quickly. Reno used its Community Development Office and City Manager's Office as areas in which to pilot the best practice, but the implementation team made it a provision that others could implement the process later on. All implementation teams can work this exporting process into the action plan.

Another aspect of exporting is the opportunity it gives an organization to institute its own team of experts. Many public organizations have established small groups of employees to serve as internal experts on quality management. Similarly any other agency can establish a team of enthusiastic benchmarkers who are familiar with the methods, benefits, and pitfalls of benchmarking. These are the resident authorities on the entire benchmarking process, an important resource in the next benchmarking project.

It may seem as if implementation is the end of the benchmarking project. It is not. The final stage in any benchmarking experience is to monitor success and sustain the improvements already made.

Chapter Eleven

Sustaining Lasting Performance Improvements

After installing a new process at five IRS service centers, the implementation team determined that the new process was not producing the anticipated results; worse, it was generating results that were poorer on the performance measures than the old process. Rather than panicking, the implementation team and the executive sponsors reviewed the identified best practice and then studied the practice as implemented in operation. They found two discrepancies between the intended process and the actual process.

First, the new process automated certain calculations that were previously done on desk calculators by tax examiners. Some of the tax examiners did not trust the computer system, so they were recalculating all of the computations. Second, the new system kept electronic versions of all the notices sent to taxpayers. The operational policy still called for paper copies of all notices to be placed in a file with all of the relevant taxpayer documents, so the tax examiners were printing copies of the notices and creating taxpayer files to store the paper notices, thus following their written procedures. The implementation team quickly addressed both of these issues, and the new process began to operate as intended. Within a few weeks the new process was outperforming the old process, and within a few months the performance measures produced with the best practice were even higher than originally anticipated.

Houston was the first major city to adopt community policing in the 1980s. More recently it has deserted the idea entirely and returned to older policing models. The new program failed in part because the Houston police force did not get the rest of the city government to buy into the community policing concept. Community policing efforts suffocate if they cannot rely on other municipal agencies for backup and support (Gurwitt, 1995, p. 21).

These experiences illustrate the difficulties organizations face in sustaining the momentum of successful best practice implementations. Just when everyone is ready to breathe a sigh of relief, declare victory, and move on, problems can occur. If they turn away from the new practice too soon, the agency may lose the opportunity for even greater learning, growth, and performance results.

Sustaining the momentum involves three types of issues: ensuring the successful implementation and operation of the new best practice in the organization, institutionalizing benchmarking as the way to search for best practices throughout the agency, and clearly defining the future of benchmarking for best practices as a means for bringing better government to citizens and customers.

Sustaining the Momentum for the New Best Practice

New processes in the organization, just like new skills we try to master, require constant attention and continual practice. The old practice must be unlearned (as old habits must be broken) and the new process exercised until it becomes standard operating procedure (just as our new skills become second nature to us; we do not even need to think about them anymore). Once a new practice identified by a benchmarking team has been implemented, the benchmarking and implementation teams, the champion, and all of the others who participated in the search, discovery, and installation of the process tend to fade away. They return to their normal jobs, move on to new benchmarking teams, or in other ways abandon the practice to survive on its own. As the two anecdotes opening this chapter point out, however, the new practice is in danger of failing if it does not continue to receive appropriate attention. Worse, the organization has missed a terrific opportunity to improve itself if it does not follow through with ongoing benchmarking activities for the new process.

Monitoring the Process

Monitoring has negative connotations for many people; it brings to mind memories of hall monitors and test monitors who watch your every move to point out your faults, lay blame, and publicly humiliate you. Although monitoring has been associated with all of these negative experiences, it can be a productive, interactive learning and growth process—a celebration of success and improvement.

Monitoring the best practice during implementation and operation is intended to be a positive learning and continual improvement experience. The benchmarking and implementation teams, the champion, the process owners, and all of the others who have participated in the search get to watch the progress of the new process as it improves performance, satisfies customers, and produces other desired results. And if the process does not perform as expected, those with the most interest in it and its results are the first to know. They are ready and able to determine why the practice is not meeting expectations and recommend modifications to ensure that it does fulfill its promise.

The steps presented in this book lay the groundwork for fairly simple, straightforward monitoring of the newly implemented best practice. The process to be benchmarked was selected on the basis of its relevance to the agency's strategic plan, goals, objectives, customer impact, and need for improvement. Performance measures were identified and data collected for both the old process and the benchmarking partners' processes. The charter for the benchmarking team stated the purpose of the benchmarking. And in the benchmarking team's final report, the team laid out the new process, performance measures for the new process, and expected results (both costs and accomplishments). All that is left is to implement the process and collect data on the performance measures.

As the best practice moves from implementation to monitoring of its operational phase, responsibility for the new process typically moves back to the line organization. Monitoring is done by closely tracking performance measures, discerning trends, and ensuring that the process continues to meet its new level of expected results. The line manager reports on these measures to the champion, the benchmarking and implementation teams, and other interested parties until the process has stabilized at its expected performance level. If problems occur or the process does not perform up to expectations, those involved in finding and implementing the practice are prepared to help address the problems. If the best practice performs as expected and stabilizes at its new performance level, the line organization begins to manage the process in its normal manner, and the functional organization becomes responsible for ongoing monitoring.

Informing the Invested Participants

Throughout the benchmarking process, many constituencies have participated, to a greater or lesser extent, in the project. Elected and appointed officials, customers and clients of the process being benchmarked, the process owners, various stakeholder or special interest groups, the champion, steering or oversight committees, the benchmarking and implementation teams, and, perhaps most important, benchmark partners have contributed time, energy, emotion, and their best thoughts to the effort. All of these participants have a vested interest in the results of the benchmarking and the monitoring of the new process in operation. It is incumbent on the organization to share results, accomplishments, and disappointments with all of these parties.

Although this task often seems somewhat onerous, especially after all the work it has taken to get this far, it provides an opportunity to share successes, learn from the difficulties encountered, reflect on what has happened, and focus on the future. Benchmarking is about learning from others' experience, and feedback about benchmarking activities allows others to learn from these experiences. Similarly, the organization that reflects on its benchmarking experience learns from its investment in the process and constantly improves its benchmarking.

Taking Advantage of the New Opportunity

Successfully implementing a best practice opens the organization to two new opportunities. First, the practice raises the performance level of the process, so the agency can recalibrate its performance measures to this new level and start the search for best practices anew. Much of the data collection, analysis, and other work from the first benchmarking study can be used to continue the search, so the renewed effort takes much less time and fewer resources. Keeping the information current and accurate makes the effort to keep the agency's practice the "best" quite easy.

The second, and more powerful, opportunity presented to the agency is to make benchmarking the normal way of doing business for the new best practice. The information is available, staff are knowledgeable, and the process owners are expected to keep the new practice best. All that needs to be done is to make this constant search for best practices the standard operating procedure for the process. With one success behind it, the organization has acquired additional experience with benchmarking, so its readiness levels have been raised. Thus the search for improvements may range further than the original study did, perhaps including more diverse organizations or dramatically different processes that can contribute to making the organization better. Success breeds success, and the search for improvement leads to a greater thirst for improvement. By encouraging, even demanding, this drive to ever-better performance, the agency builds its power to address other processes and improve the services it provides its customers.

Sustaining the Momentum for Benchmarking

Just as the organization has identified and implemented a new best practice successfully, it has also successfully defined and exercised the benchmarking process itself. And benchmarking, like any other process, should be documented, measured, and improved. The champion, the benchmarking team, and, to a lesser extent, the implementation team and process owners are responsible for these activities.

A simple model for organizational learning posits four steps in the learning process. In the first stage, the initial experience, the participants undoubtedly made some mistakes, had some unexpected successes, and encountered new challenges and surprises. These experiences should not be taken lightly; they are the basis for organizational learning.

In the second phase of the learning process, the benchmarking participants individually and collectively reflected on what these experiences, trials, tribulations, and accomplishments meant to them, the organization, and its customers. It is often very helpful to include benchmarking partners and stakeholders in the reflection process. Many organizations skip this stage, preferring to use a "ready, fire, aim" approach to improvement. These organizations believe they have had twenty years of experience and are pretty good at what they do; in fact, they have had the same experience twenty times and are no better now than when they first went through it. All participants need to take time to understand the benchmarking experience; benchmarking takes an agency through the process and ends with a new experience that builds on the past rather than repeating it.

When the benchmarking experience has been reflected on and understood, the agency is ready to make decisions about how to improve the process. The beginning of this step is to carefully and clearly articulate decision criteria and the impact of the decisions on customers and on performance of the process. The final stage is to implement the changes as aggressively as the implementers installed the best practice. This step may be the most challenging because it requires breaking the comfort and inertia established in a successful benchmarking effort. Implementing thoughtful changes is the only way to ensure a new experience during the next benchmarking project, however; otherwise the same experience will be repeated over and over.

The new, improved benchmarking process is then documented, measures are established, and the process used to find a new best practice. As with any other process undergoing improvement, the benchmarking process improvement effort is more likely to succeed if it receives the proper support. The naming of a champion and a process owner for the benchmarking process helps to communicate the importance of, and establishes clear responsibility for, improving the process itself. Implementing performance measures for the process demonstrates that it will be treated like any other organizational process. It also lays the framework for data-based decision making on the process, continuing improvement, and a search for best practices. After all, benchmarking is a process that can be benchmarked as well. The exciting challenge here is to work with benchmarking partners to find the best benchmarking process and to improve that process continually, use the benchmarking to reach higher and higher levels of performance, and find new and better ways to delight taxpayers, customers, and elected and appointed representatives.

Preparing for the Future of Benchmarking

The forces driving public sector agencies to find best practices will only become more intense. The public will become more demanding; the need for excellence will become even greater. Budgets will shrink, the demand for accountability in the public sector will increase, the need for demonstrable results will grow, and taxpayer frustration, even outrage, will sweep the country like wildfire.

Officials in the public sector must respond to these pressures with positive, results-oriented actions designed to resolve the issues, not find excuses or become apologists for ineffectiveness. If we in the public sector continue down the path we have followed, we are destined to become a smaller and less significant part of the American scene. We will continue to be seen as part of the problem, the cause of what is wrong with the country, rather than a part of the solution. Our challenge is to deliver timely, high-quality products and services that delight customers and overwhelm elected and appointed officials with their measurable results.

Over the years we have worked with many organizations and watched many others as they tried to respond to this pressure to perform. Some organizations withdraw into themselves. A bunker mentality sets in, and the world comes to be seen as divided between us and them. Other organizations turn outward, looking for help, ideas, and new perspectives from outside their own boundaries. Benchmarking encourages agencies to look outward. It provides the reasons and methods that organizations need to seek out best practices and solve their performance problems.

As a history of successful benchmarking is written in an agency, the search for best practices grows wider, the striving for improvement becomes constant, and a culture of customer-focused improvement develops. The IRS has ten service centers located across the country responsible for processing tax returns, correspondence, and other taxpayer account issues. These centers have built a foundation for continual improvement. They have defined their processes, developed and implemented performance measures, and experienced both incremental and breakthrough process improvements. In 1992 the IRS service center in Ogden received the President's Award for Quality. In the true spirit of benchmarking, the other centers identified and imported best practices from Ogden, and Ogden sought out and found best practices in some of the other centers. In the ensuing years several other centers also received the President's Award. The culture of the centers is now one marked by a continual search for improvement and an eager willingness to share best practices with partner organizations. The drive for excellence in one organization feeds a similar drive in the other organizations in an upward spiral of ever-improving performance.

Benchmarking is not a panacea, the solution to all of the problems public sector agencies face, but it is a powerful weapon in the performance improvement arsenal. Technology gives us immediate and easy access to people, places, organizations, and experiences throughout the world, providing us with a vast amount of information and resources. We have a worldwide network in which to seek out common problems and uncommon solutions. Sharing experiences and learning from the experiences of other organizations is the cheapest and most efficient, effective, and compelling means for improving performance. Benchmarking provides the approach, methodology, tools, and techniques to maximize the value of this exchange of information.

We in the public sector face unprecedented challenges that provide almost unlimited opportunities to excel. The search for best practices, the use of benchmarking in pursuit of new and better ways to fulfill our public mandate, is a clear path to performance improvement that will thrill citizens. In the process, it can also bring unexpected renewal and enthusiasm to public servants and focus the energy of the public and our private sector partners in a collaborative effort to improve government and its institutions.

Benchmarking Resources

By now you are undoubtedly contemplating how you might identify, import, and sustain the kinds of organizational improvements achieved by West Virginia and Salt Lake City. The methodology and real-life examples presented in this book will help you determine if benchmarking can lead your organization to breakthrough performance. As with any new exercise, putting benchmarking methodology into practice can create moments of uncertainty.

This section, which consists of checklists and descriptions of key tools, complements the descriptions of methodology provided earlier in the book. The checklists, which are based on years of benchmarking practice, will ensure a smooth road as you forge a partnership that is likely to be different from any you have previously experienced.

Benchmarking in the Knowledge Era: On-Line Resources and Other Research Tools

Although the benefits of discovering, analyzing, and implementing best practices are inescapable, it should be noted that benchmarking can represent a significant investment of both human and financial resources. The issue is not how to minimize the investment, but rather how your organization can leverage the investment to maximum advantage. The key, we believe, lies in a concept commonly referred to as *knowledge management*.

The idea is that organizations are composed not of *things* but of *people,* and that the people employed by an organization collectively represent an organization's intellectual capital, its intangible pool of skill, knowledge, and information. An organization that effectively engages in knowledge management seeks to ensure that the intellectual capital possessed by one or more employees in one unit or division is shared with employees in other units and divisions. This sort of knowledge sharing leads to what many notable thinkers have called "*learning organizations—* organizations that are capable of creating, acquiring, and transferring knowledge and of modifying behavior across divisional boundaries to reflect new knowledge and insight" (Garvin, 1993, pp. 80–81).

Learning organizations typically have five characteristics:

1. They are adept at solving problems.
2. They encourage experimentation with new approaches.
3. They develop and maintain methods for learning from past experiences.
4. They support the exercise of learning from the best practices of others.
5. They are adept at transferring knowledge quickly and efficiently throughout the organization.

Learning organizations are ones in which valuable insights are routinely shared throughout the system, enabling even far-flung divisions to pick up, expand on, implement, and communicate back the results of an improvement or a new development. Such knowledge sharing continually raises the bar of performance across the entire organization and ensures that it will remain agile—that is, constantly behave in a proactive manner, providing products and services that are increasingly customized to the needs of its customers.

What does it take to be a learning organization? As it becomes more and more a part of our daily lives, technology acts as both a conduit through which we interact with others during a benchmarking exercise and a channel through which best practices and lessons learned are shared across organizations. Technology provides opportunities to share both "explicit knowledge (formal and systematic knowledge relating to things like product specifications, formulas, and software programs) and tacit knowledge (knowledge that is highly personal, such as that which is related to skills or techniques)" (Nonaka, 1991, p. 98). In this section, we will explore ways to use technology both to learn about best practices and to share knowledge throughout an agency.

Information Mining: Public Domain Research

The recent proliferation of databases and on-line services has provided today's benchmarkers with the informational equivalent of FAO Schwarz, a veritable toyland full of opportunities to access publicly available data. The challenge now is to engage in effective and efficient "information mining," a term referring to the exercise of finding and managing appropriate data sources and repositories.

The exponential growth of the Internet, a nonproprietary, publicly available information superhighway that links sites throughout the world, allows just about anyone to engage in data gathering. Key word searches including the word *benchmarking* can connect you to all manner of benchmarking clubs and networks, many of which offer their own proprietary databases. Beyond ease of access, the Internet assures exposure to data that is global in nature. That means that your team can gain insights far beyond your national boundaries.

For example, a trip along the superhighway may result in a visit to Sandia Labs, where you will learn about agile and advanced manufacturing. You may pop in on the CIO 100 Winners list to see what is happening in information technology around the world. Or try visiting the Eli Broad Graduate School at Michigan State University in Lansing to learn about best practices in global logistics. Because German manufacturers are known to approach world-class status (frequently integrating cradle-to-grave designs and green product capabilities), a visit to the Benchmarking Information Center of Germany may prove fruitful. Or better yet, why not partner with one of Germany's government relations or regulatory agencies to see how they support German companies in complying with regulatory requirements? All this for the price of dialing up!

Beyond the Internet, there is a multitude of other places to shop for data. Whatever the scope of your project, there is likely to be a benchmarking database or clearinghouse that caters to your needs. Organizations sponsoring best practice clearinghouses include Software Productivity Research, The Benchmarking Exchange (TBE), the U.S. Department of Labor, and the United States Navy. The Edgar database, created and maintained by the U.S. Securities and Exchange Commission, provides information on corporate filings.

Directories, both published and on-line, are another valuable source of information. *Inside UK Enterprise,* for example, a directory compiled by the Department of Trade and Industry in the United Kingdom, lists companies throughout the UK willing to share best practices. Listings include basic company data (such as location and employee head count) as well as best practices (such as collections systems and mortgage front-end processing), issues they would like to explore with other companies, and dates during which site visits will be sponsored. Hoover's produces a whole series of directories, published by Reference Press, Inc., in hard copy, CD, and on-line formats, representing a rich source of company data including telephone numbers.

One mistake beginning benchmarkers often make is immediately attempting to partner with award-winning companies such as Malcolm Baldrige National Quality Award winners without conducting appropriate research. Effectively mining for information ensures that your team gains access to data that is most relevant to the project at hand.

Information Mining: Interactive Benchmarking

Because of its nearly real-time communications capability, the Internet offers value beyond the preliminary research phase. At the most basic level, the Internet supports the ability to communicate through electronic mail anywhere in the world almost instantaneously. E-mail can be used during every stage of the benchmarking process, to solicit partner involvement, to exchange site visit plans, and to distribute final reports.

At the more sophisticated end of the spectrum, through increasingly common programming techniques, agencies or organizations with a World Wide Web site can create a page that both captures data from benchmarking partners and provides immediate feedback on where those data stand in relation to the general field of partners.

Take the case of a university whose goal is to compare its core process indicators with those of the competition. It creates an on-line survey instrument and invites partners to feed their core process indicators into the instrument. With the click of a mouse, both parties are able to assess where the subject stands against the overall field of benchmarking partners. Interactive benchmarking not only saves time, it allows each partner to produce its own report and often eliminates the need for a costly site visit.

Leveraging Intellectual Capital

The increasing popularity of "groupware" and "Intranet" software—technologies that enable employees within an organization to communicate and share data in a real-time environment—demonstrates the power of knowledge management. A new policy implemented in the St. Louis office of the Internal Revenue Service, for example, can be made available to the entire organization by posting it on an electronic bulletin board or by publicizing it on a "desktop."

One professional services firm, for example, initiated a knowledge network composed of virtual television channels. Users tune into an internal "channel" to participate in a dialogue or sharing session. E-Systems, an electronics company based in Dallas, Texas, developed a system called ECLIPSE, allowing access to internal and external information. The system scans documents, accepts data from CD-ROMs, and provides access to electronic publications and subscription databases. Users can search by key words and view lists of topics accompanied by abstracts. A full article can be accessed by clicking on the abstract.

Knowledge sharing does not require technology. In fact, almost any organization can realize significant benefits from some old-fashioned networking. One way to network within your agency is to publish a directory listing employees' areas of expertise, phone numbers, mail stations, and any other means of contact (for example, E-mail). Organizations that encourage knowledge sharing will often have some centralized database (this can be electronic or on paper) that tracks the activities of continuous improvement teams, benchmarking teams, reengineering teams, and so on. The challenge is to encourage employees to tap into the vast resource of information and lessons learned that the database represents.

A 1994 study conducted by INSEAD, the European Institute of Business Administration in Fontainebleau Celex, France, reveals that best-performing companies are the most likely to implement best practices that have been communicated within the organization. Worst companies are the next likely candidates, followed in last place by the middle-of-the-road companies, which undoubtedly engage in the knowledge transfer process only as a result of internal peer pressure.

Without effectively managing the intellectual capital that is the very foundation of all organizations, no agency can hope to justify its existence. To be a learning organization is to embrace aggressively the tools of breakthrough improvement and leverage the results across the enterprise.

Directory of Benchmarking and Best Practices Organizations

Air Combat Command
205 Dodd Boulevard, Suite 100
Langley Air Force Base
Langley, VA 23665–2788
Tel.: (804) 764–3204
Fax: (804) 764–3589

Air Force Standard Systems Center
Department of the Air Force
Department of Defense
The Pentagon
Washington, DC 20301
Tel.: (703) 545–6700

Alliance for Redesigning Government
David Osborne, Chairman
National Academy of Public Administration
1120 G Street, N.W., Suite 850
Washington, DC 20005–3801
Tel: (202) 347–3190
Fax: (202) 393–0993
E-mail: napa@tmn.com

American Institute of Certified Public Accountants
Harborside Financial Center
201 Plaza Three
Jersey City, NJ 07311–9811
Tel: (212) 596–6200
Fax: (212) 596–6213

American Productivity and Quality Center
123 North Post Oak Lane, Third Floor
Houston, TX 77024–7797
Tel.: (800) 776–9676
Fax: (713) 681–5321
E-mail: apqcinfo@apqc.org

American Society of Public Administration
1120 G Street, N.W.
Washington, DC
Tel.: (202) 393–7878
Fax: (202) 638–4952
E-mail: dcaspa@ix.netcom.com

American Society for Quality Control (ASQC)
611 East Wisconsin Avenue
P.O. Box 3005
Milwaukee, Wis. 53201–3005
Tel: (800) 248–1946
Fax: (414) 272–1734
Quality Information Center, ext. 8693
Homepage: http://www.asqc.org

Arlington County, Virginia
Homepage: http://www.co.arlington.va.us
Department of Community Planning, Housing and Development
Susan Ingraham, Zoning Administrator
2100 Clarendon Boulevard, Suite 812
Arlington, VA 22201
Tel.: (703) 358–3883
Fax: (703) 358–3896

Department of Economic Development
Gene Davis, Productivity Analyst
2100 Clarendon Boulevard, Suite 700
Arlington, VA 22201
Tel: (703) 358–3808
Fax: (703) 358–3574

Fire Department
Edward P. Plaugher, Fire Chief
2100 Clarendon Boulevard, Suite 400
Arlington, VA 22201
Tel.: (703) 358–3355
Fax: (703) 358–7097

Benchmarking Competency Center
American Society for Quality Control
611 East Wisconsin Avenue
P.O. Box 3005
Milwaukee, WI 53201–3005
Tel.: (800) 248–1946
Fax: (414) 272–1734
Homepage: http://www.asqc.org

The Benchmarking Exchange, Inc.
7960-B Soquel Drive, Suite 536
Aptos, CA 95003
Tel.: (408) 662–9800
Fax: (408) 662–9800
E-mail: TBE@benchnet.com

Carl Bertelsmann Prize
Bertelsmann Stiftung
Carl-Bertelsmann-Strabe 256
33311 Gutersloh
Germany
Tel.: (05241) 7406–29
Fax: (05241) 73882

Best Practices in Missouri Schools
Missouri Council of School Administrators
MCSA Outreach
P.O. Box 1117
Columbia, MO 65205–1117
Tel.: (314) 499–1840
Fax: (314) 499–1844
Homepage: http://www.services.dese.state.mo.us/bestpractices

City of Arlington, Texas
Parks and Recreation Department
P.O. Box 231
Arlington, TX 76004–0231
Tel.: (817) 459–5474
Fax: (817) 459–5495

City of Charlotte, North Carolina
Customer Service Center
Dottie Disher, Manager
Office of the City Manager
600 East Fourth Street
Charlotte, NC 28202
Tel.: (704) 336–7600

City of Lynchburg, Virginia
Fire and Emergency Services Department
800 Madison Street
Lynchburg, VA 24504
Tel.: (804) 847–1602
Fax: (804) 846–6727

City of Phoenix, Arizona
City Auditor Department
17 South Second Avenue, Suite 200
Phoenix, AZ 85003
Tel.: (602) 262–6641
Fax: (602) 534–1533

Public Information Office
251 West Washington Street
Phoenix, AZ 85003
Tel.: (602) 262–7176
Fax: (602) 495–2432

City of Reno, Nevada
Carol Peterson, Management Analyst
P.O. Box 1900
Reno, NV 89505
Tel.: (702) 334–2285 (A.M.)
(702) 334–2018 (P.M.)

City of Salt Lake, Utah
Brenda R. Hancock, Manager
Employment, Compliance and Training
451 South State Street, Room 404
Salt Lake City, UT 84111
Tel.: (801) 535–6307

City of Seattle, Washington
Customer Service Bureau
Terry Wittman, Director
105 Municipal Building
600 Fourth Avenue
Seattle, WA 98104
Tel.: (206) 684–8818

Department of Neighborhoods
Jim Diers, Director
400 Artic Building
700 Third Avenue
Seattle, WA 98104–1848
Tel.: (206) 684–0464
Fax: (206) 233–5142

Community Policing Consortium
1726 M Street, N.W., Suite 801
Washington, DC 20036
Tel.: (202) 833-3305
Fax: (202) 833-9295

Department of Veterans Affairs (VA)
810 Vermont Avenue, N.W.
Washington, DC 20420
Tel: (202) 273-5400

Milton S. Eisenhower Foundation
1660 L Street, N.W., Suite 200
Washington, DC 20036
Tel.: (202) 429-0440
Fax: (202) 452-0169

Exemplary State and Local Award (EXSL)
National Center for Public Productivity
Dr. Marc Holzer, Director
Rutgers University
Graduate Department of Public Administration
360 King Boulevard
Hill Hall 701
Newark, NJ 07102
Tel.: (201) 648-5093
Fax: (201) 648-5907
E-mail: mholzer@andromeda.rutgers.edu

William G. Gay
Public Management Group
12015 Sugarland Valley Drive
Herndon, VA 22070-2604
Tel.: (703) 478-0980
Fax: (703) 478-0981

General Services Administration
18th and F Streets, N.W.
Washington, DC 20405
Tel.: (202) 708–5082
Office of Public Affairs
Tel.: (202) 501–0705
Fax: (202) 501–1300

Governing
Congressional Quarterly Inc.
2300 N Street, N.W., Suite 760
Washington, DC 20037
Tel.: (202) 862–8802
Fax: (202) 862–0032

Hackett Group
1691 Georgetown Road
Hudson, OH 44236
Tel.: (216) 656–3110
Fax: (216) 463–5471

Innovation Group
Mark Glover, Director
P.O. Box 16645
Tampa, FL 33687–6645
Tel.: (813) 622–8484
Fax: (813) 664–0051
E-mail: tcgk02c@prodigy.com

Innovations in American Government Awards
John F. Kennedy School of Government
Harvard University
Taubman Center for State and Local Government
79 JFK Street
Cambridge, MA 02138
Tel.: (800) 722–0074
Fax: (617) 496–4602
Homepage: http://ksgwww.harvard.edu/^innovat/

International Association of Fire Chiefs
4025 Fair Ridge Drive
Fairfax, VA 222033–2868
Tel.: (703) 273–0911
Fax: (703) 273–9363

International Benchmarking Clearinghouse
American Productivity and Quality Center
123 North Post Oak Lane, Third Floor
Houston, TX 77024–7797
Tel.: (800) 776–9676
Fax: (713) 681–5321
E-mail: apqcinfo@apqc.org

International Institute for Learning (IIL)
110 East 59th Street, Sixth Floor
New York, NY 10022–1380
Tel.: (212) 758–0177
Fax: (212) 909–0559
E-mail: info@iil.com

Malcolm Baldrige National Quality Award
U.S. Department of Commerce
Technology Administration
National Institute of Standards and Technology
Route 270 and Quince Orchard Road
Administration Building, Room A537
Gaithersburg, MD 20899–0001
Tel.: (301) 975–2036
Fax: (301) 963–0339
E-mail: oqp@nist.gov

Milwaukee, Wisconsin, Fire Department
Bureau of Administration
711 West Wells Street
Milwaukee, WI 53233
Tel.: (414) 286–8948
Fax: (414) 286–8996

National Academy of Public Administration
1120 G Street, N.W., Suite 850
Washington, DC 20005–3801
Tel.: (202) 347–3190
Fax: (202) 393–0993
E-mail: napa@tmn.com

National Center for Public Productivity
See under "Exemplary State and Local Award"

National Performance Review
750 17th Street, N.W.
Washington, DC
Tel.: (202) 632–0150
Fax: (202) 632–0390
Homepage: http://www.npr.gov

New York City Transit Authority
Executive Office
370 J Street, Suite 1300
Brooklyn, NY 11201
Tel.: (718) 330–3000
Fax: (718) 596–2146

Oregon Shines
Oregon Progress Board
Oregon Economic Development Department
775 Summer Street, N.E.
Salem, OR 97310
Tel.: (503) 986–0039
Fax: (503) 581–5115
Homepage: http://lidmail.chemek.cc.or.us/^rig/opb/index.htm

Portland, Oregon, Fire Department
3200 Southeast Harrison Street
Portland, OR 97222
Tel.: (503) 786–7400
Fax: (503) 786–7426

Prince George's County, Maryland, Police Department
7600 Barlowe Road
Palmer Park, MD 20785
Tel.: (301) 336–8800
Fax: (301) 772–4788

Public Innovator Learning Network
John Scully, Manager
National Academy of Public Administration
1120 G Street, N.W., Suite 850
Washington, DC 20005–3801
Tel.: (202) 383–7774
Fax: (202) 347–3252
E-mail: jscully217@aol.com
Homepage: http://www.clearlake.ibm/com/Institute/.
Fax on demand: (800) 344–7853

Public Management Group
William G. Gay, President
12015 Sugarland Valley Drive
Herndon, VA 22070–2604
Tel.: (703) 478–0980
Fax: (703) 478–0981

Public Sector Network
American Society of Public Administration
1120 G Street, N.W.
Washington, DC 20005
Tel.: (202) 393–7878
E-mail: dcaspa@ix.netcom.com

Quality Progress
American Society for Quality Control (ASQC)
611 East Wisconsin Avenue
P.O. Box 3005
Milwaukee, WI 53201–3005
Tel.: (800) 248–1946
Fax: (414) 272–1734
Homepage: http://www.asqc.org

John Scully
See under "Public Innovator Learning Network"

Standard Reporting of Performance Measures
See under "Innovation Group"

U.S. Conference of Mayors
1620 I Street, N.W.
Washington, DC 20006
Tel.: (202) 293–7330
Fax: (202) 293–2352

West Virginia INSPIRE Initiative
Rebecca Davison, Project Coordinator
Office of the Governor
Charleston, WV 25305
Tel.: (304) 558–7995

Division of Labor
State Capitol Complex
Building 3, Room 319
Charleston, WV 25305
Tel.: (304) 558–7890

Division of Tourism
2101 Washington Street, East
Charleston, WV 25305–0312
Tel.: (304) 558–2200

Division of Motor Vehicles
State Capitol Complex
Building 3, Room 113
Charleston, WV 25305
Tel.: (304) 558–2723

Step-by-Step Checklists for Managing a Benchmarking Project

Getting Started

Identifying the Process to Benchmark

The first step in any project is to identify the process to be benchmarked. As discussed earlier in this book, not every process is an appropriate subject for this methodology. The following questions will help you determine which processes are the best benchmarking candidates:

- Does the process have a high impact on customer or constituent satisfaction (directly or indirectly)?
- Does the process consume a significant amount of employee time?
- Does the process consume a significant amount of its customers' or constituents' time?
- Does the process have a high impact on the budget?
- Does the process yield quantifiable defects?
- Does the process rely on several vertical levels of the organization?
- Does the process feature non-value-added steps such as delays, inspections, storage, transportation, rework?
- Does the process support your business mission and impact your return on assets?

Creating the Project Description

Once the core process to be benchmarked has been identified, a project description or study format of one to two pages should be drafted. This brief report functions as both a mechanism through which to obtain approval from more senior-level executives and a preliminary communication link to your team's champion, who will most likely be somewhat distanced from the project on a day-to-day basis. Although there are as many formats to use for the project overview as there are processes, a good project description should contain the following elements:

- A full definition of the process to be benchmarked
- The name(s) of the process owner(s)
- Project justification, with supporting data
- Long-term and short-term goals of the study in quantifiable terms
- Scope of the project
- Criteria used to select partners
- Duration of the project
- Team members
- Critical metrics to be compared
- Benefits to the agency as well as the benchmarking team
- Units, divisions, or processes affected by the project

Initiating the Partnership

Identifying Potential Partners

Whether you are benchmarking internally with other units or divisions within your agency or externally in public services or the private sector, your team will have to consider potential partners through a variety of filters. The first filter is innovation. Following are some guidelines to use in identifying potential partners whose practices are truly innovative. A practice, method, or process may be a best practice if it

- Yields results at least 25 percent higher than average output
- Demonstrates an innovative use of manpower or technology
- Is recognized by at least three different public domain references
- Has achieved external recognition in the form of an award
- Has achieved recognition by customers or suppliers

- Has been recognized by an independent industry expert
- Has been awarded a patent
- Contributes to exceptional performance

The second filter concerns relevance. It requires asking questions about how a potential partner compares with your agency. Possible questions include

- How many people do they employ?
- Do we provide similar products or services?
- Are we both centralized (decentralized)?
- Are our customers' or constituents' expectations similar?
- Do we occupy the same market sector (for example, education, military)?

Finally, you will want to gauge accessibility of data on each potential partner. Issues to consider include

- Is this organization known to monitor the types of data in question?
- What is the likely cost of visiting and collecting data from this agency?
- Are there any legal barriers to sharing data?
- Is the organization likely to invest resources (human and financial) in sharing information?

Making Contact with Potential Partners

As benchmarking gains in popularity, best practice companies often find themselves flooded with requests to share information. The right preparation for your initial contacts will ensure that your request is considered and will increase your chances of a successful partnership. Following are some examples of the types of information potential partners will expect you to furnish during your initial contact:

- Name and description of your agency
- Name and description of the process/function/area to be studied
- Goals and purpose of the study
- Intended use of the information to be obtained
- Reason for targeting the potential partner

- Other targeted agencies and/or companies to be contacted
- Current status of your study
- Current status of your internal analysis
- Methods for documenting your process
- Key performance metrics associated with the study
- Status and nature of questionnaire development
- Desired time frame and project schedule
- Suggested formats for exchanging information (questionnaire, telephone interview, site visits)
- Limits or restrictions on information exchange and suggested terms for confidentiality
- Intentions regarding adherence to the Benchmarking Code of Conduct
- Involvement of external consultants, if any
- Advantages of participation to the targeted agency (for example, sharing of final report, opportunities for reciprocal exchange)

Developing the Questionnaire

The partner questionnaire, the final filter applied to a partner prior to a site visit, is a critical step in the benchmarking project and should be constructed with care. Because questionnaire development is an art, it is worthwhile to seek the help of an appropriately skilled group or department within your own agency (for example, market research or technical publications) or to hire an external consultant specializing in surveys. Following are areas you will want to explore through the survey instrument:

- Key measurements used to monitor the process
- Any current problems experienced in the process
- Recent or planned improvements made to the process
- Critical process enablers
- Planned process enhancements

The Site Visit

Planning the Visit

A visit to your benchmarking partner's site is a lot like the inspection of a home you are about to purchase; the obvious difference is that you will not buy the partner, but rather may borrow elements of its process. As with a home inspection, you will want to spend considerable time preparing for a site visit to ensure that the time and money invested on both sides of the relationship yield valuable and relevant information. An effective way to do this is to draw up a site visit plan. Following are items to consider in creating the plan:

- Develop, prioritize, and test questions to be asked during the site visit.
- Determine how critical data will be collected during the visit.
- Assign roles and responsibilities to all members of the benchmarking team.
- Study the Benchmarking Code of Conduct.
- Create and share a site visit agenda with your partner(s) prior to the visit.
- Develop a brief opening presentation, to include the study mission and objectives, an overview of your agency, and brief introductions of all team members.

Conducting the Site Visit

With effective planning and preparation, the actual site visit will be a stress-free and rewarding event. Following are some tips to get the most out of the visit:

- Stick to the agenda.
- Bring plenty of business cards, paper and writing instruments, and a copy of the benchmarking protocol with you.
- Maintain a friendly, professional tone.
- Always keep flowcharts and process information handy, both as reference and to share with your partner.
- Schedule frequent breaks for team members to caucus.
- During team caucuses, determine if the site visit objectives are being met.
- Maximize the sharing of data and observations by holding a team meeting immediately upon leaving the site.
- Send a thank you note to your partner immediately on return to your home base.

Implementing Best Practice Recommendations

Prioritizing Implementation Criteria

Before you plan wholesale implementation of your best practice recommendations, it is wise to step back and weigh the projected payoffs against the investment required. Prioritizing criteria for implementation will ensure that your plan is aligned with your organization's readiness for the changes required. For each criterion considered, project both positive and negative consequences of implementation. See Table C.1 for sample criteria and projected consequences.

Creating an Action Plan

An implementation plan should include both the steps that lead to realization of the best practice as well as steps detailing how the process will be monitored once the practice is implemented. As discussed earlier in this book, walking away from the job once the practice has been implemented is tantamount to bringing a child into the world and assuming that without supervision he or she will turn out just fine. The following steps should be integrated into your flowcharted plan:

- Develop a milestone chart.
- Implement the practice.
- Document results achieved to date as compared with plan.
- Document implementation problems.
- Document deviations from plan.
- Document corrective actions taken.
- Document successes and improvements.

Successful implementation entails not only focusing on the process at hand but understanding and preparing for consequences that will be outside of the benchmarking team's control. Following are additional issues to consider as you draft your implementation action plan:

- Have all tasks been disaggregated with specified results?
- Have tasks been sequenced?

- Have necessary resources been secured for each task?
- Has the plan in its entirety been communicated to management?
- Has the plan been communicated to affected individuals, both within the process in question and in processes upstream and downstream?

Table C.1. Prioritized Implementation Criteria: Sample.

Criterion	Consideration	Projected Consequences
Process improvement	To what degree will it affect the quality and productivity of the process?	• Will reduce cycle time by x days • Will improve customer satisfaction by factor of x
Implementation timeframe	How long will it be before results will be achieved, and what will be the impact the current process?	• Implementation will take x weeks • The current process will experience downtime of x hours
Resources	How many and which people (internal and external) and what additional tools are required to implement?	• x software developers • x external consultants • x existing personnel
Cost	What is the projected cost of implementation?	• x new kiosks/terminals/PCs required at a cost of $\$x$ • x hours of training at a cost of $\$x$ per day • x days of training time for personnel at a cost of $\$x$
Training	What specialized training is required? Of whom? How long will it take?	• x customer service attend half-day workshop
Risks	What risks have been considered, and what is the probable result?	• Possible system downtime of x hours at a cost to service centers of $\$x$

Recommended controls	How will implementation be monitored to minimize risks?	• Introduction of new programming to occur on weekend, supervised by a team of developers, programmers, operators
Personnel implications	What personnel changes are indicated?	• Hire x developers • Promote x customer service reps • Decrease supervisor staff by x • Total change in head count of $\$x$
Up/downstream impact	What other processes will be affected by implementation?	• Paper supplier will have to deliver just-in-time • 1040 processing team will receive x more files per day

Key Benchmarking Tools

Just as carpenters require certain tools to turn ideas into reality, benchmarkers rely on a set of tools to transform processes into best practices. The most fundamental way to think about benchmarking tools is as a set of measuring sticks. For benchmarking is, after all, based on our ability to measure, improve, and measure again.

The first three tools described here are fundamental and can be used in a variety of quality-oriented applications. Because benchmarking is ultimately designed to create improvements of an order of magnitude that far outstrips those seen with sustained continuous improvement efforts, we have included two tools (spider charts and Z charts) that are a little more advanced. We suggest concentrating on the first three tools initially and then adopting tools four and five to maximize the potential outcome of your benchmarking project. Collectively, these tools will enable your team to realize "leapfrog" improvements that will ensure that your agency remains competitive.

Functional Process Flowcharts

Stated simply, flowcharts are the blueprints of your process. To begin a benchmarking project without process flowcharts would be akin to renovating a house without drawing blueprints of the existing structure. Functional process flowcharts fulfill a variety of functions, at least two of which are fundamental to benchmarking. First, they provide an understanding of a process both at the detailed task level and at an overview level that shows the implications for those upstream and downstream of the process. Second, they permit a comparison of one's own process to those of bench-marking partners.

A flowchart will document inputs (things or data that are generated by an internal or external supplier), process (what happens to the inputs), outputs (things or data that are produced by the process), and results (the experience of the internal or external customer). Figure D.1 shows the most basic universal flowchart symbols.

Simply documenting this flow can yield actionable observations. Perhaps there is unnecessary redundancy. Or inputs may be coming from an indirect supplier. Try comparing the number of boxes on your flowchart with those on your partners' charts. (But make sure that the process is broken down to the same sublevel tasks.) You may find that your partner is able to conduct the same fundamental process with significantly fewer steps.

There are currently several software packages designed to turn input into flowcharts. Most are easy to use and take the guesswork out of turning data into visual images.

Matrix Analysis

Matrices are an effective way to identify how various benchmarking partners compare with one another in a variety of dimensions. Each benchmarking partner is listed on one axis of the matrix (in a blinded study, partners will be identified as partner A, partner B, and so on). The other axis features each of the metrics in question. Data on each metric are then plotted onto the matrix. Once this picture is created, one or more organizations will usually stand out as demonstrating superior performance. These companies or agencies are prime targets for a benchmarking project. It is also useful to consider how your process compares with those of the potential partners; you may find that your process is better than you think. Table D.1 shows an example of a matrix analysis.

Matrices can also be used to help a group of senior officials or department heads achieve consensus on just which processes should be benchmarked. Once the group agrees on the business priorities for the entire organization, these can be listed on one axis, while processes owned by the participants can be listed on the other. The group then discusses which processes have the greatest overall impact on each business priority.

Figure D.1. Universal Flowchart Symbols.

- **Ovals** are used to indicate the start or end point of a process.

  Start

- **Rectangles** represent steps or activities that are placed in sequence from top to bottom or left to right.

  Create taxpayer file

- **Arrows** demonstrate sequence and lead the way to the next work step or destination in the process.

- **Diamonds** represent decision or approval points. They are generally followed by two decision paths.

  Taxes computed correctly?   Yes

  No

- **Circles** indicate inspection points.

  Inspect files

- **Inverted triangles** represent storage.

  Store in file

- **Outline arrows** indicate movement or transportation.

  Ship to processing center

Table D.1. Sample Matrix Analysis: Order-Picking Data.

	Company A	Company B	Company C	Company D
Line picks per month	49,000	32,000	12,000	150,000
Picks per operator hour	25	30	75	56
Number of parts per line pick	2.5	5	3	12
Number of expedited orders per day	25	80	30	76
Cycle time (days) from order to delivery	2	7	5	4.5
Inventory turns per year	4	6	12	7

Gap Analysis

Gap analysis, a tool enabling teams to assess the degree of difference between processes, can be used to identify the performance gaps between your process and the best practice. Gap analysis generally makes use of a matrix that shows critical metrics along one axis and actual performance measures on the other. This tool allows a benchmarking team to understand the performance measures of potential partners as a percentage (positive or negative) of its own. Table D.2 provides an example of gap analysis.

Spider Charts

One challenge often confounding benchmarking teams is how to compare processes involving more than one critical measure. Spider charts, which require that data be normalized (that is, translated to one common measure such as percentage), offer a solution.

Table D.2. Sample Gap Analysis: Order-Picking Data.

	Home Process	Company B	Percent + or −	Company C	Percent + or −
Line picks per month	49,000	32,000	−35%	12,000	−76%
Picks per operator hour	25	30	+20%	75	+300%
Number of parts per line pick	2.5	5	+100%	3	+20%
Number of expedited orders per day	25	80	+320%	30	+20%
Cycle time (days) from order to delivery	2	7	+350%	5	+250%
Inventory turns per year	4	6	+50%	12	+200%

Teams begin by drawing a circle with various spokes, each of which represents one critical measure. Data points from the home process are plotted on the diagram and connected. Then data points from benchmarking partners (one at a time) are plotted and connected, a different color or type of line being used for each partner. Gaps between the home process and that of the partners are easily identifiable. Figure D.2 shows an example of a spider chart.

Eastman Kodak, a pioneer in the application of spider charts in benchmarking, was honored with an International Benchmarking Clearinghouse award for this practice. The company uses spider charts to project how a change in one variable is likely to affect the remaining variables in a process. As your team creates implementation recommendations, try plotting projected outcomes for each critical measure and determining how these changes will affect the

Figure D.2. Sample Spider Chart.

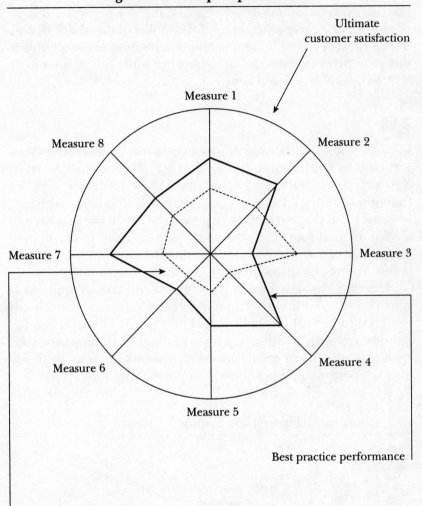

overall process. You might find that some measures will significantly improve whereas others diminish, resulting in a process problem, or bubble, that gets pushed around the spokes of the wheel. By contrast, you want to implement changes that either cause all indicators to improve or cause some to improve while others, which are already desirable, remain constant.

Z Charts

Industry and competitive performance do not stagnate while your team is busy implementing a best practice. Z charts, pioneered by Xerox, help benchmarking teams describe performance gaps as a function of time. This tool is used both to demonstrate the performance gap that currently exists between the home process and that of the best practice (or industry average) and to predict the magnitude of the performance gap that will exist after implementation. Figure D.3 shows an example of a Z chart.

Once you have determined the time it will take to implement your changes, your team can identify the rate of improvement required to both close the gap and surpass the best practice (or industry average). Nothing is quite as motivating as comparing your agency's status quo or even planned incremental gains to the breakthrough performance achieved by implementing a best practice.

Figure D.3. Sample Z Chart.

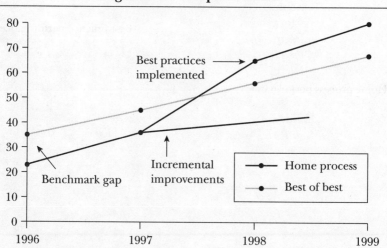

References

American Productivity and Quality Center. *American Productivity and Quality Center: Who We Are.* Houston, Tex.: American Productivity and Quality Center, n.d.

Anthes, G. H. "White House Gets Tech Advice." *Computerworld,* 1993, *27*(31), 4.

Anthes, G. H. "Agencies Earn System Awards." *Computerworld,* 1994, *28*(32), 16.

Barrett, K., and Greene, R. "Focus on the Best." *Financial World,* Mar. 2, 1993, pp. 36–55.

Barvenik, T., and Davis, G. Interview with P. Keehley and S. MacBride, Arlington, Va., June 9, 1995.

"Benchmarking Code of Conduct, Etiquette Guidelines, Exchange Protocol, and Ethical and Legal Guidelines." *Quality Management Forum,* 1994, *20*(3), 15–17.

Bruder, K. A., Jr., and Gray, E. M. "Public-Sector Benchmarking: A Practical Approach." *Public Management,* 1994, *76*(9), S9–S22.

Camp, R. C. *Benchmarking: The Search for Industry Best Practices That Lead to Superior Performance.* Milwaukee, Wis.: ASQC Quality Press, 1989a.

Camp, R. C. "Benchmarking: The Search for Best Practices That Lead to Superior Performance, Part II." *Quality Progress,* Feb. 1989b, pp. 70–75.

Carr, D. K., and Littman, I. D. *Excellence in Government: Total Quality Management in the 1990s.* Arlington, Va.: Coopers & Lybrand, 1990.

Cartwright, P. "Benchmarking Measures of Customer Service Sites." Video presentation, Breakthrough Results with Benchmarking Conference, New York, June 27, 1995.

Coopers & Lybrand. *Best Practices of Improvement Driven Organizations: How Today's High Performers Produce Results.* Arlington, Va.: Coopers & Lybrand, n.d.

Doades, R. "Making the Best of Best Practices." *Public Utilities Fortnightly,* 1992, *130*(4), 15–18.

Ernst & Young LLP and American Quality Foundation. *The International Quality Study—Best Practices Report: An Analysis of Management Practices*

That Impact Performance. Cleveland, Ohio: Ernst & Young LLP and American Quality Foundation, 1993.

"Fire Services Performance Reporting and Benchmarking." Announcement of a conference held June 14–15, 1995, sponsored by the International Association of Fire Chiefs, Northern Virginia Community College, Management Development Center, and local fire departments.

Fischer, R. J. "An Overview of Performance Measurement." *Public Management,* 1994, *76*(9), S2–S8.

Garvin, D. A. "Building a Learning Organization." Harvard Business Review, July–Aug. 1993, pp. 80–81.

Gay, W. "Benchmarking: A Method for Achieving Superior Performance in Fire and Emergency Medical Services." Herndon, Va.: Public Management Group, 1992.

General Accounting Office. *Executive Guide: Improving Mission Performance Through Strategic Information Management and Technology.* Report GAO/AIMD-94–115. Washington, D.C.: U.S. Government Printing Office, 1994.

General Accounting Office (National Security and International Affairs Division). *Best Practices Methodology: A New Approach for Improving Government Operations.* Report GAO/NSIAD-95–154. Washington, D.C.: U.S. Government Printing Office, 1995.

"Governing for Results: Using Benchmarks to Define and Measure Progress Toward Strategic Priorities." Prepared for the Association of Oregon Counties, July 21, 1994.

Gurwitt, R. "Cops and Community." *Governing,* May 1995, p. 21.

Hackett Group. *AICPA/THG Benchmark Study: Results Update and Analyses.* Cleveland, Ohio: Hackett Group, 1994.

Hatry, H., and Kirlin, J. J. *An Assessment of the Oregon Benchmarks: A Report to the Oregon Progress Board.* Washington, D.C.: Urban Institute, 1994.

Heller, B. *Benchmarking: City of Arlington, Texas, Parks and Recreation Department.* Arlington: City of Arlington, Texas, Parks and Recreation Department, 1994.

"Innovation Group's Standard Reporting of Performance Measures: Factsheet, Instructions and Sample Data Sheets." Memo. Arlington County, Va., n.d.

International Institute for Learning. *Breakthrough Results with Benchmarking.* Pamphlet for the Breakthrough Results with Benchmarking Conference, New York, N.Y., June 27, 1995.

Janofsky, M. "Baltimore Journal: Japanese-style Booths Put Police at the Center of the Action." *New York Times,* July 31, 1995.

Jeter, J. "The Mixed Success of Community Policing." *Washington Post,* Oct. 31, 1995, p. C1.

Keehley, P. *Benchmarking Customer Service: Site Visits to Charlotte and Seattle.* Arlington, Va.: iKon Group, inc., 1995.

Kwok, A. "Phoenix Sitting on Top of World As Best-Run City." *Arizona Republic,* Sep. 9, 1993, pp. A1, A9.

Lawrence, B. "Problem Solving: Revenue Canada Shares Best Practices Electronically." *Leader's Digest,* 1994, *8*(3), 22. Internal Revenue Service, Office of Internal Communications, Document 7168.

Moe, R. "What Does 'Employee Involvement' Mean?" *Public Administration Review,* 1995, *28*(7), 67–71.

National Academy of Public Administration. *Public Innovators Information Cooperative.* Washington, D.C.: National Academy of Public Administration, Alliance for Redesigning Government, n.d.

National Center for Public Productivity. *Site Visit Policy and Instructions* [and evaluation forms]. Newark, N.J.: Rutgers University, National Center for Public Productivity, Exemplary State and Local Awards Program, May 16, 1995.

National Institute of Standards and Technology. *Malcolm Baldrige National Quality Award 1995 Award Criteria.* Gaithersburg, Md.: U.S. Department of Commerce, National Institute of Standards and Technology, 1995.

National Performance Review. *From Red Tape to Results: Creating a Government That Works Better and Costs Less.* New York: Random House, 1993.

National Performance Review. *Serving the American Public: Best Practices in Telephone Service.* Washington, D.C.: U.S. Government Printing Office, 1995.

"News Report." *Journal of Accountancy,* 1993, *175*(5), 15–16.

Nonaka, I. "The Knowledge-Creating Company." *Harvard Business Review,* Nov.–Dec. 1991, p. 98.

Oregon Department of Administrative Services. *Choices for Oregon's Future: 1995–1997. Budget and Legislative Proposal Instructions.* Salem: Oregon Department of Administrative Services, Fiscal Policy Analysis Division, n.d.

Oregon Economic Development Department. *Oregon Shines: An Economic Strategy for the Pacific Century—Summary.* Salem: Oregon Economic Development Department, 1989.

Oregon Progress Board. *Oregon Benchmarks: Standards for Measuring Statewide Progress and Institutional Performance.* Report to the 1995 Legislature. Salem: Oregon Progress Board, 1994.

Osborne, D., and Gaebler, T. *Reinventing Government: How the Entrepreneurial Spirit Is Transforming the Public.* Reading, Mass.: Addison-Wesley, 1992.

Overman, E. S., and Boyd, K. J. "Best Practices Research and Post-bureaucratic Reform." *Journal of Public Administration Research and Theory,* 1994, *4*(1), 67–83.

"Performance and Democracy in Local Government: Carl Bertelsmann Prize, 1993." Press release. Phoenix: City of Phoenix, Arizona, Public Information Office, n.d.

Plaugher, E. P. Interview with S. MacBride, Arlington, Va., July 14, 1995.

Public Management Group. *Benchmarking Law Enforcement Services.* Herndon, Va.: Public Management Group, n.d.

Public Management Group. "Fire and Emergency Medical Survey." Survey form prepared for the city of Lynchburg, Virginia. Herndon, Va.: Public Management Group, n.d.

Public Management Group. *Fire/EMS Benchmarks: Lynchburg, Va.* Herndon, Va.: Public Management Group, n.d.

Public Management Group. *Program Performance Measurement: Exploring the User's Need to Know.* Herndon, Va.: Public Management Group, n.d.

Public Sector Network News (American Society for Quality Control). Summer 1994.

Scully, J. Interview with P. Keehley and S. MacBride, Washington, D.C., July 21, 1995.

Senge, P. *The Fifth Discipline: The Art and Practice of the Learning Organization.* Garden City, N.Y.: Doubleday, 1990.

"This Year's Carl Bertelsmann Prize Awarded to Christchurch, New Zealand, and Phoenix, Arizona, USA." Press release. Gutersloh, Germany: Bertelsmann Stiftung, Sept. 8, 1993.

U.S. Conference of Mayors. *Publications.* Washington, D.C.: U.S. Conference of Mayors. Office of Public Affairs, 1995.

"Use TQM, Benchmarking to Improve Productivity." *Public Relations Journal,* 1994, *50*(1), vii.

Vaziri, H. K. "Using Competitive Benchmarking to Set Goals." *Quality Progress,* Oct. 1992, pp. 81–85.

Weisendanger, B. "Benchmarking Intelligence Fuels Management Moves." *Public Relations Journal,* Nov. 1993, pp. 20–22.

West Virginia Benchmarking Project. *Measuring Customer Satisfaction: Report to the Governor.* Charleston, W.V.: Feb. 1996.

Index